THE ESSENTIAL

Dachshund

The Dachshund's Senses

SIGHT

Dachshunds can detect movement at a greater distance than we can, but they can't see as well up close. They can also see better in less light, but can't distinguish many colors.

SOUND

Dachshunds can hear about four times better than we can, and they can hear high-pitched sounds especially well.

SMELL

A Dachshund's nose is his greatest sensory organ. A dog's sense of smell is so great he can follow a trail that's weeks old. Because the Dachshund is a scent-hound, his nose is usually on the ground and his sense of smell is especially on track.

TASTE

Dachshunds have fewer taste buds than we do, so they're likelier to try anything—and usually do, which is why it's important for their owners to monitor their food intake. Dogs are omnivorous, which means they eat meat as well as vegetables.

TOUCH

Dachshunds are social animals and love to be petted, groomed and played with.

CHAPTER ONE

Getting to Know Your Dachshund

The Dachshund is not a quiet addition to a home: He wants to be with you! Anywhere you go, he will go; any place you sit will be just perfect for him; anything you're eating will be fine, thank you. He is comical without planning to be, protective when he feels he needs to be and solicitous when he senses things are not quite right in your world. His world, however, is fine as long as you are in it!

EXPECT THE UNEXPECTED

What can you expect from this alert little hound? The unexpected! Remembering that he is a scenthound will save you a lot of aggravation. His nose is extraordinary! Dachshunds can smell paper-towel tubes in a wastepaper basket, a speck of food under a cabinet, a crumb, well aged, behind the refrigerator. If he tells you something is lurking beyond your sight, believe him.

Dachshunds are curious about everything.

This delightful little hound is, however, a dichotomy. While he keeps you guessing and will always surprise you, he is predictable and single-minded. What he likes, he will always like; habits once ingrained, stick. However, he has a mind of his own, and he uses it. He will outsmart you with great glee anytime the chance arises.

So, what can you expect from your Dachshund? Loyalty. Love. Humor. Agility. Curiosity. Intelligence.

A HUNTING HOUND

The Dachshund is a sturdy hunting hound. He comes in two sizes—Standard and Miniature. Even the Miniature is not a fragile animal. Small is not a word in the Dachshund's vocabulary. In addition to the two sizes, the Dachshund also comes in three coat varieties—smooth (short hair), long- and wire-haired.

Your Dachshund will hunt just about anything. Scents appeal to him. That's what he was bred to do. So, off he will go, following a scent—most likely your scent—straight to your shoes or your clothes or your mattress or to food! It is much easier to keep things away from him than to keep him away from things. Remember that. It will save you a lot of aggravation and a lot of money!

Never forget your Dachshund is a scent hunter and should never be off leash unless he has thorough obedience training. Once he gets the scent, he is single-minded and will be off. Off lead, this hound, in almost any instance, is not trustworthy unless trained to respond to your verbal or signaled commands. He may stay by your side or never leave your property nine times out of ten, but he is not by nature a stay-at-home dog; if he picks up a scent, he'll track it!

It is difficult to keep this breed's nose from the grass. Summer shows present a problem if they are held outdoors, and many obedience people prefer the fall and winter shows held on cement floors. However, in the conformation ring, a dropped piece of liver will pull that head and nose to the floor in a second! Yet, as active as this hound is, he is a lapdog, a sleep-next-to-you-in-the-chair dog, a curl-up-at-your-feet-in-the-bed dog.

This hound is also persistent. He'll bark at the garbage until you remove it. He will jump on the furniture no matter how many times you tell him "No!"—unless you remain firm and do not give in. Being opinionated, he will test you. Being sly, he will do it if he thinks you're not

around. Being intelligent, he will get down when he hears you coming or if you are forceful in your command to "Get off the sofa!"

QUICK, PLAYFUL, HUNGRY!

Despite the jokes made about his shape, the Dachshund is quick and agile. Chasing and running after him is a no-win situation! Standing still is good, because if you feign interest in something, his curiosity will eventually win out and he'll usually give up the cat-and-mouse game and come to investigate.

This little dog loves toys and balls and paper-towel tubes and will

Dachshunds like to be with their favorite people.

3

When a Dachs-hund picks up an interesting scent, he'll definitely investigate.

amuse himself for hours if his people won't play with him. Expect your Dachshund to beg if you don't train him not to do so. He is a chowhound, and more often than not he will eat anything. He will steal, given the chance, and be a pest if allowed. Ban him from the kitchen or dining room until you have trained him to stay away from the table. "Stay!" is a good command to teach early!

The Dachshund is not normally a one-person dog, though he may prefer some family members over others. A well-bred Dachshund's temperament is cordial and outgo-ing. He is slightly wary of strangers and makes an excellent watchdog. Properly introduced to children, he accepts them willingly and makes an ideal companion for them. Common sense is the secret here. Children who are young should be supervised; older children should be educated in the proper and considerate ways of handling a dog.

It will be up to you to make sure guests who are welcomed to your home are introduced to your Dachshund. He is an alert watchdog and needs to be told it is all right for this person to come into his domain. A puppy that has been properly socialized will make a gentle, loving companion who will readily accept anyone you accept.

Be careful that your dog does not slip out the door while you are greeting guests, as he might take off unless he has been trained.

The Dachshund loves to see what is going on around him. He is very rarely a sideliner, a bystander or a wallflower. What goes on on his front lawn, his street, next door or down the block is part of his territory. He watches and he listens and he barks! Persistent training will curb this, but no one will sneak up on you unawares.

CHARACTERISTICS OF THE DACHSHUND

Curious

Agile

Single-minded

Comical

Fearless

Sturdy

Scent hunter

This lively hound is not an outdoors-only dog. Tied up, he will bark his head off. He will gnaw

Dachshunds are smart dogs; sometimes they test the rules of the house.

Dachshunds love to play with their toys.

The Dachshund is a clean dog, easily housebroken if trained with praise and encouragement. As a breed, they want to please you and don't respond readily to harsh methods.

The coat is easily maintained, with the longhairs and the soft-coated wires needing more attention than the smooths and wires with the correct rough coat.

Once trained to walk on the lead, until age slows him down, this alert inquisitive hound loves walks and hikes through the woods, around the neighborhood or down the street. Remember, always keep your Dachshund on the leash unless trained to obey the basic commands.

through any rope, and left out for long periods in a fenced area, he will dig his way under!

A FAITHFUL COMPANION

The Dachshund is a people dog. He'll stay where you are and go where you go. When he is with you, he will be content. If he knows you're coming back, he will wait patiently. But he won't be the kind of dog you can pat on the head and then leave to go off and do other things. He will demand his share of your attention, and he will delight you with the warmth of his welcome.

Are there downsides? Of course, the Dachshund is active. He can be strong-willed, if you allow it. Bored, he can get into mischief. He loves to burrow under blankets and under anything you put on the chair to protect the upholstery. If you allow him to share your bed, no matter now large it is, you'll find yourself curled up near the edge as he spreads out under the covers!

Once you are owned by a Dachshund, you will never come into a room or a house you've left, even if

Your Dachshund will appreciate your attention and companionship.

it was only to take out the garbage or bring in the newspaper, without this delightful little hound greeting you with his tail beating the floor, so delighted to see you, so happy you've returned to his world.

CHAPTER TWO

Homecoming

B efore bringing home your new family member, a little planning can help make the transition easier. The first decision to make is where the puppy will live. Will she have access to the entire house or be limited to certain rooms? A similar consideration applies to the yard. It is simpler to control a puppy's activities and to housetrain the puppy if she is confined to definite areas. If doors do not exist where needed, baby gates make satisfactory temporary barriers.

A dog crate is an excellent investment and is an invaluable aid in raising a puppy. It provides a safe, quiet place where a dog can sleep. Used properly, a crate helps with housetraining. However, long periods of uninterrupted stays are not recommended—especially for young puppies. Unless you have someone home or can have someone come in a few times a day to let her out to relieve herself and socialize with her for a while, a *small* crate is not advisable. Never lock a young puppy in a small crate for an entire day!

PUPPY-PROOFING

It is definitely easier to raise a puppy than a human being, but many of the same precautions should be taken. While puppies cannot open cabinets or stick their paws in light sockets, they can get in a lot of trouble with very little effort. Place anything that might be susceptible to puppy teeth or could be broken out of their reach. If possible, all electrical cords should be hidden or secured to floors and walls. Unfortunately such things as tables and chairs cannot be kept out of reach of puppy teeth. If your puppy takes an interest in these, you can buy bitter-tasting sprays to apply to these surfaces.

Puppies also get into harmful substances. Anything that is poisonous to humans will harm a dog. Antifreeze tastes sweet and is deadly to animals. Most garden sprays, snail baits and rat poisons are toxic to dogs, so they must be kept out of reach and used with extreme caution. Other things to watch out for are the plants in the yard and in the house.

There are even things that do not bother humans that are dangerous for dogs. Two of these items are chocolate and some salmon. Both are potentially poisonous to dogs

PUPPY ESSENTIALS

To prepare yourself and your family for your puppy's homecoming, and to be sure your pup has what she needs, you should obtain the following:

Food and Water Bowls: One for each. We recommend stainless steel or heavy crockery—something solid but easy to clean.

Bed and/or Crate Pad: Something soft, washable and big enough for your soon-to-be-adult dog.

Crate: Make housetraining easier and provide a safe, secure den for your dog with a crate—it only looks like a cage to you!

Toys: As much fun to buy as they are for your pup to play with. Don't overwhelm your puppy with too many toys, though, especially the first few days she's home. And be sure to include something hollow you can stuff with goodies, like a Kong.

I.D. Tag, inscribed with your name and phone number.

Collar: An adjustable buckle collar is best. Remember, your pup's going to grow fast!

Leash: Style is nice, but durability and your comfort while holding it count, too. You can't go wrong with leather for most dogs.

Grooming Supplies: The proper brushes, special shampoo, toenail clippers, a toothbrush and doggy toothpaste.

9

A dog crate will provide your Dachshund with a safe place to rest or play.

and should be kept away from your Dachshund.

TOYS AND ACCESSORIES

Excessive chewing can be partially resolved by providing a puppy with her own chew toys. Latex toys, paper-towel tubes and toilet-tissue tubes are also great favorites with Dachshunds, who love to toss them around! Anything given to a dog must be large enough that it cannot be swallowed. It is best to provide a puppy with a few choice toys rather than too many.

As a puppy matures and gets her adult teeth, a variety of items made of hard nylon compounds and in a variety of shapes can provide endless hours of chewing fun. Rawhide chews should be given with caution. Some dogs are over-zealous in trying to swallow the chewed pieces, and, if large enough, these pieces can get lodged in the throat.

Your puppy will need a close-fitting, adjustable nylon collar. A properly fitted collar is tight enough that it will not slip over the head, yet an adult finger fits easily under it. A puppy should never wear a choke chain or any other adult training collar.

In addition to a collar, you'll need a 4-to-6-foot-long leash. One made of nylon or cotton-webbed material is fine as an inexpensive first leash. It need not be more than $1/2$ inch in width. It is important to make sure that the clip is of excellent quality and cannot become unclasped on its own.

The final starter items a puppy will need are a water bowl and food dish. Stainless-steel bowls or crock dishes are good and long-lasting; plastic of any sort is quickly chomped

on by this breed. For some of these clever hounds, a weighted water bowl is advisable—some of them enjoy turning them over.

THE ALL-IMPORTANT ROUTINE

Most puppies do best if their lives follow a schedule. They need definite and regular periods of time for playing, eating and sleeping. Puppies like to start their day early. This is a good time to take a walk or play some games of fetch. After breakfast, most are ready for a nap. How often this pattern is repeated will depend on one's daily routine. Sometimes it is easier for a working person or family

11

Protect your curious new puppy by puppy-proofing your home prior to her homecoming.

HOUSEHOLD DANGERS

Curious puppies and inquisitive dogs get into trouble not because they are bad, but simply because they want to investigate the world around them. It's our job to protect our dogs from harmful substances, like the following:

In the Garage

antifreeze

garden supplies, like snail and slug bait, pesticides, fertilizers, mouse and rat poisons

In the House

cleaners, especially pine oil

perfumes, colognes, aftershaves

medications, vitamins

office and craft supplies

electric cords

chicken or turkey bones

chocolate, onions

some house and garden plants, like ivy, oleander and poinsettia

to stick with a regular schedule than it is for someone who is home all of the time.

Most dogs reach their peak of activity and need the least amount of rest from 6 months to 3 years of age. As they mature, they spend increasingly longer periods of time sleeping. It is important to make an effort to ensure that a Dachshund receives sufficient exercise each day to keep her in proper weight and fitness throughout her life. Puppies need short periods of exercise, but, due to the fact that their bodies are developing, it should never be done to excess. Walks are more suitable for Dachshunds than running.

PROTECTIVE MEASURES

It is *vital* that your dog always wear some sort of ID. The rabies tag alone is useless, since it can't be traced

Your puppy will need some chew toys to keep her occupied.

should your dog get lost. Your pet's ID tag should contain your pet's name as well as your name and phone number. The Dachshund Club of America has a rescue representative in almost every part of this country. If you lose your Dachshund, call the American Kennel Club and they can put you in touch with someone in your area (or the area where your Dachshund was lost) who will be only too willing to help you and get the word out to be on the lookout for your pet.

The single best preventative measure that one can take to ensure that a dog is not lost or stolen is to provide her with a completely fenced-in yard. Check the fence periodically for digging spots or weakened structure.

IDENTIFY YOUR DOG

It is a terrible thing to think about, but your dog could somehow, someday, get lost or stolen. For safety's sake, every dog should wear a buckle collar with an identification tag. A tag is the first thing a stranger will look for on a lost dog. Inscribe the tag with your name and phone number.

There are two ways to permanently identify your dog. The first is a tattoo, placed on the inside of your dog's thigh. The tattoo should be your social security number or your dog's AKC registration number. The second is a microchip, a rice-sized pellet that is inserted under the dog's skin at the base of the neck, between the shoulder blades. When a scanner is passed over the dog, it will beep, notifying the person that the dog has a chip. The scanner will then show a code, identifying the dog.

13

Providing your Dachshund with a completely fenced-in yard is the best way to keep her from being lost or stolen.

CHAPTER THREE

To Good Health

up to us to take preventive measures to make sure that none of these interferes with our dog's health. It may help to think of the upkeep of a dog's health in relation to the calendar. Certain things need to be done on a weekly, monthly and annual basis.

PREVENTIVE HEALTH CARE

Weekly grooming can be the single best monitor of a dog's overall health. The actual condition of the coat and skin and the "feel" of the body can indicate good health or potential problems. Grooming will help you discover small lumps on or under the skin in the early stages before they become large enough to be seen without close examination.

The strongest body and soundest genetic background will not help a dog lead a healthy life unless he receives regular attention from his owner. Dogs are susceptible to infection, parasites and diseases for which they have no natural immunity. It is

You may spot fleas and ticks when brushing the coat and examining the skin. Besides harboring diseases and parasites, they can make daily life a nightmare for some dogs. Some Dachshunds are allergic to even a couple of fleas on their bodies. They scratch, chew and destroy their coat and skin because of fleas.

Flea Control

Flea control is never a simple endeavor. Dogs bring fleas inside, where they lay eggs in the carpeting and furniture—anywhere your dog goes in the house. Consequently, real control is a matter of not only treating the dog but also the other environments the flea inhabits. The yard can be sprayed, and in the house, sprays and flea bombs can be used, but there are more choices for the dog. Flea sprays are effective for one to two weeks. Dips applied to the dog's coat following a bath have equal periods of effectiveness. The disadvantage to both of these is that some dogs may have problems with the chemicals.

Flea collars prevent the fleas from traveling to your dog's head, where it's moister and more hospitable. Dog owners tend to leave flea collars on

Your regular attention and preventive mesures will go a long way in keeping your Dachshund healthy.

15

FLEAS AND TICKS

There are so many safe, effective products available now to combat fleas and ticks that—thankfully—they are less of a problem. Prevention is key, however. Ask your veterinarian about starting your puppy on a flea/tick repellent right away. With this, regular grooming and environmental controls, your dog and your home should stay pest-free. Without this attention, you risk infesting your dog and your home, and you're in for an ugly and costly battle to clear up the problem.

Run your hands regularly over your dog to feel for any injuries.

16

their dogs long after they've ceased to be effective. Again, some dogs may have problems with flea collars, and children should never be allowed to handle them.

Some owners opt for a product that works from the inside out. One such option is a pill (prescribed by a veterinarian) that you give to the dog on a regular basis. The chemicals in the pill course through the dog's bloodstream, and when a flea bites, the blood kills the flea.

Another available option is a product that comes in capsule form. The liquid in the capsule is applied near the dog's shoulders, close to the skin where it distributes into the skin and coat to protect against fleas and ticks. Ask your veterinarian about this nontoxic, long-lasting tick and flea preventative.

Ticks

As you examine your dog, check also for ticks that may have lodged in his skin, particularly around the ears or in the hair at the base of the ear, the armpits or around the genitals. If you find a tick, which is a small insect about the size of a pencil eraser when engorged with blood, smear it with petroleum jelly. As the tick suffocates, it will back out and you can then grab it with tweezers and kill it. If the tick doesn't back out, grab it with tweezers and gently pull it out, twisting very gently. Don't just grab and pull or the tick's head may remain in the skin, causing an infection or abscess for which veterinary treatment may be required.

A word of caution: Don't use your fingers or fingernails to pull out ticks. Ticks can carry a number of diseases, including Lyme disease, Rocky Mountain spotted fever and others, all of which can be very serious.

Proper Ear Care

Another weekly job is cleaning the ears. Many times an ear problem is evident if a dog scratches his ears or shakes his head frequently. Clean ears are less likely to develop problems, and if something does occur, it will be spotted while it can be treated easily. If a dog's ears are very dirty and seem to need cleaning on a daily basis, it is a good indication that something else is going on in the ears besides ordinary dirt and the normal accumulation of earwax. A visit to the veterinarian may indicate a situation that needs special attention.

Brushing Teeth

Regular brushing of the teeth often does not seem necessary when a dog is young and spends much of his time chewing; the teeth always seem to be immaculately clean. As a dog ages, it becomes more important to brush the teeth daily.

To help prolong the health of your dog's mouth, he should have his teeth cleaned twice a year at a veterinary clinic. Observing the mouth regularly, checking for the formation of abnormalities or broken teeth, can lead to early detection or oral cancer or infection.

Keeping Nails Trimmed

The nails on all feet should be kept short enough so they do not touch the ground when the dog walks.

Use tweezers to remove ticks from your dog.

Check your dog's teeth frequently and brush them regularly.

Dogs with long nails can have difficulty walking on hard or slick surfaces. This can be especially true of older dogs. As nails grow longer, the only way the foot can compensate and retain balance is for the toes themselves to spread apart, causing the foot itself to become flattened and splayed.

Nails that are allowed to become long are also more prone to splitting. This is painful to the dog and usually

YOUR PUPPY'S VACCINES

Vaccines are given to prevent your dog from getting infectious disease like canine distemper or rabies. Vaccines are the ultimate preventive medicine: They're given before your dog ever gets the disease so as to protect him from the disease. That's why it is necessary for your dog to be vaccinated routinely. Puppy vaccines start at 8 weeks of age for the five-in-one DHLPP vaccine and are given every three to four weeks until the puppy is 16 months old. Your veterinarian will put your puppy on a proper schedule and will remind you when to bring in your dog for shots.

18

requires surgical removal of the remainder of the nail for proper healing to occur.

Keeping Eyes Clear

A Dachshund's eyes sometimes need special attention. A small amount of matter in the corner of the eye is normal, as is a bit of "tearing."

Dachshunds with eyelashes that turn inward and rub against the eye itself often exhibit more tearing than normal due to the irritation to the eyes. These eyelashes can be surgically removed if they appear to be a problem, but are often ignored.

Excessive tearing can be an indication that a tear duct is blocked. This, too, can be corrected by a simple surgical procedure. Eye discharge that is thicker and mucous-like in consistency is often a sign of some type of eye infection or actual injury to the eye. This can be verified by a veterinarian, who will provide a topical ointment to place in the corner of the eye. Most minor eye injuries heal quickly if proper action is taken.

VACCINES

All dogs need yearly vaccinations to protect them from common deadly diseases. The DHL vaccine, which protects a dog from distemper, hepatitis and leptospirosis, is given for the first time at about 8 weeks of age, followed by one or two boosters several weeks apart. After this, a dog should be vaccinated every year throughout his life.

Since the mid-1970s, parvovirus and coronavirus have been the cause of death for thousands of dogs. Puppies and older dogs are most frequently affected by these illnesses. Fortunately, vaccines for these are now routinely given on a yearly basis in combination with the DHL shot—the combined shot is referred to as the five-in-one DHLPP.

Kennel cough, though rarely dangerous in a healthy dog that receives proper treatment, can be annoying. It can be picked up anywhere that large numbers of dogs congregate, such as veterinary clinics, grooming shops, boarding kennels, obedience classes and dog shows. The Bordatella vaccine, given twice a year, will protect a dog from getting most strains of kennel cough. It is often not routinely given, so it may be necessary to request it.

INTERNAL PARASITES

While the exterior part of a dog's body hosts fleas and ticks, the inside of the body is commonly inhabited by a variety of parasites. Most of these are in the worm family. Tapeworms, roundworms, whipworms, hookworms and heartworm all plague dogs. There are also several types of protozoa, mainly *coccidia* and *giardia,* that cause problems.

The common tapeworm is acquired by the dog eating infected fleas or lice. Normally one is not aware that a healthy dog even has tapeworms, The only clues may be a dull coat, a loss of weight despite a good appetite

or occasional gastrointestinal problems. Confirmation is by the presence of worm segments in the stool. These appear as small, pinkish-white, flattened rectangular-shaped pieces. When dry, they look like rice. If segments are not present, diagnosis can be made by the discovery of eggs when a stool sample is examined under a microscope. Ridding a dog temporarily of tapeworm is easy with a worming medicine prescribed by a veterinarian. Over-the-counter wormers are not effective for tapeworms and may be dangerous. Long-term tapeworm control is not possible unless the flea situation is also handled.

Ascarids are the most common roundworm (nematode) found in dogs. Adult dogs that have roundworms rarely exhibit any symptoms that would indicate the worm is in their body. These worms are cylindrical in shape and may be as long as 4 to 5 inches. They do pose a real danger to puppies, where they are usually passed from the mother through the uterus to the unborn puppies.

It is wise to assume that all puppies have roundworms. In heavy infestations, they will actually appear in the puppy stools, though their

19

All puppies should be checked for roundworms.

presence is best diagnosed by a stool sample. Treatment is easy and can begin as early as 2 weeks of age and is administered every two weeks thereafter until eggs no longer appear in a stool sample or dead worms are not found in the stool following treatment. Severely infected puppies can die from roundworm infestation. Again, the worming medication should be obtained through a veterinarian.

Hookworm is usually found in warmer climates and infestation is generally from ingestion of larvae from the ground or penetration of the skin by larvae. Hookworms can cause anemia, diarrhea and emaciation. As these worms are very tiny

and not visible to the eye, their diagnosis must be made by a veterinarian.

Whipworms live in the large intestine and cause few if any symptoms. Dogs usually become infected when they ingest larvae in contaminated soil. Again, diagnosis and treatment should all be done by a veterinarian. One of the easiest ways to control these parasites is by picking up stools on a daily basis. This will help prevent the soil from becoming infested.

The protozoa can be trickier to diagnose and treat. Coccidiosis and giardia are the most common, and primarily affect young puppies. They are generally associated with overcrowded, unsanitary conditions and can be acquired from the mother (if she is a carrier), the premises themselves (soil) or even water, especially rural puddles and streams.

The most common symptom of protozoan infection is mucous-like, blood-tinged feces. It is only with freshly collected samples that diagnosis of this condition can be made. With coccidiosis, besides diarrhea, the puppies will appear listless and lose their appetites. Puppies often harbor the protozoa and show no symptoms unless placed under stress. Consequently, many times a puppy will not become ill until he goes to his new home. Once diagnosed, treatment is quick and effective and the puppy returns to normal almost immediately.

Heartworm

The most serious of the common internal parasites is the heartworm. A dog that is bitten by a mosquito infected with the heartworm *microfilaria* (larvae) will develop worms that are 6 to 12 inches long. As these worms mature they take up residence in the dog's heart.

The symptoms of heartworm may include coughing, tiring easily, difficulty breathing and weight loss. Heart failure and liver disease may eventually result. Verification of heartworm infection is done by drawing blood and screening for the microfilaria.

In areas where heartworm is a risk, it is best to place a dog on a preventative, usually a pill given once a month.

At least once a year, a dog should have a full veterinary examination. The overall condition of the dog can be observed and a blood sample collected for a complete yearly screening. This way, the dog's thyroid function can be tested, and the job the dog's organs are doing can be monitored. If there are any problems, this form of testing can spot trouble areas while they are easily treatable.

Proper care, regular vaccinations, periodic stool checks and preventative medications for such things as heartworm will all help ensure your dog's health.

SPAYING/NEUTERING

Spaying a female dog or neutering a male is another way to make sure they lead long and healthy lives. Females spayed at a young age have almost no risk of developing mammary tumors or reproductive problems. Neutering a male is an excellent solution to dog aggression and also removes the chances of testicular cancer.

Female Dachshunds usually experience their first heat cycle somewhere between 6 months and 1 year of age. Unless spayed they will continue to come into heat on a regular cycle. The length of time between heats varies, with anything from every six months to a year being normal.

There is absolutely no benefit to a female having a first season before being spayed, nor in letting her have a litter. The decision to breed any dog should never be taken lightly. The obvious considerations are whether he or she is a good physical specimen of the breed and has a sound temperament. There are genetic problems that are common to Dachshunds, such as disc disease. Responsible breeders screen for these prior to making breeding decisions.

Finding suitable homes for puppies is another serious consideration. Due to their popularity, many people are attracted to Dachshunds and seek puppies without realizing the drawbacks of the breed.

Regular vaccinations, preventive medications and proper care will help keep your Dachshund healthy.

Owning a dog is a lifetime commitment to that animal. There are so many unwanted dogs—and yes, even unwanted Dachshunds—that people must be absolutely sure that they are not just adding to the pet overpopulation problem. When breeding a litter of puppies, it is more likely that you will lose more than you will make, when time, effort, equipment and veterinary costs are factored in.

COMMON PROBLEMS

Not Eating or Vomiting

One of the surest signs that a Dachshund may be ill is if he does not eat. That is why it is important to know your dog's eating habits. For most dogs, one missed meal under normal conditions is not cause for alarm, but more that that and it is time to take your dog to the veterinarian to search for reasons. The vital signs should be checked and gums examined. Normally, a dog's gums are pink; if ill, they will be pale and gray.

There are many reasons why dogs vomit, and many of them are not cause for alarm. You should be concerned, however, when your dog vomits frequently over the period of

ADVANTAGES OF SPAY/NEUTER

The greatest advantage of spaying (for females) or neutering (for males) your dog is that you are guaranteed your dog will not produce puppies. There are too many puppies already available for too few homes. There are other advantages as well.

Advantages of Spaying

No messy heats.

No "suitors" howling at your windows or waiting in your yard.

No risk of pyometra (disease of the uterus) and decreased incidences of mammary cancer.

Advantages of Neutering

Decreased incidences of fighting, but does not affect the dog's personality.

Decreased roaming in search of bitches in season.

Decreased incidences of many urogenital diseases.

a day. If the vomiting is associated with diarrhea, elevated temperature and lethargy, the cause is most likely a virus. The dog should receive supportive veterinary treatment if recovery is to proceed quickly.

Get to know your Dachshund's eating habits—if he starts missing meals, he may be ill.

Vomiting that is not associated with other symptoms is often an indication of an intestinal blockage. Rocks, toys and clothing will lodge in a dog's intestine, preventing the normal passage of digested foods and liquids.

If a blockage is suspected, the first thing to do is an x-ray of the stomach and intestinal region. Sometimes objects will pass on their own, but usually surgical removal of the object is necessary.

Diarrhea

Diarrhea is characterized as very loose to watery stools that a dog has difficulty controlling. It can be caused by anything as simple as changing diet, eating too much food, eating rich human food or having internal parasites.

First try to locate the source of the problem and remove it from the dog's access. Immediate relief is usually available by giving the dog an intestinal relief medication, such as Kaopectate or Pepto-Bismol. Use the same amount per weight as for humans. Take the dog off his food for a day to allow the intestines to rest, then feed meals of cooked rice with bland ingredients added. Gradually add the dog's regular food back into his diet.

If diarrhea is bloody or has a more offensive odor than might be expected and is combined with vomiting and fever, it is most likely a virus and requires immediate veterinary attention. If worms are suspected as the cause, a stool sample should be examined by a veterinarian and treatment to rid the dog of the parasite should follow when the dog is back to normal. If allergies are suspected, a series of tests can be given to find the cause. This is especially likely, if after recovery and no other evidence of a cause exists, a dog returns to his former diet and the diarrhea recurs.

Dehydration

To test your dog for dehydration, take some skin between your thumb and forefinger and lift the skin upward gently. If the skin does not go back to its original position quickly, the Dachshund may be suffering from dehydration. Consult your veterinarian immediately.

Poisoning

Vomiting, breathing with difficulty, diarrhea, cries of pain and abnormal body or breath odor are all signs that your pet may have ingested some poisonous substance. Poisons can also be inhaled, absorbed through the skin or injected into the skin, as in the case of a snakebite. Poisons require professional help without delay!

Broken Bones

If your dog breaks a bone, immobilize the limb very carefully, and seek veterinary help right away. If you suspect a spinal injury, place the dog on a board very slowly and carefully tie him securely to the board before immediately transporting him to the veterinarian.

POISON ALERT

If your dog has ingested a potentially poisonous substance, waste no time. Call the National Animal Poison Control Center hot line:

(800) 548-2423 ($30 per case) or

(900) 680-0000 ($20 first five minutes; $2.95 each additional minute)

Some of the many household substances harmful to your dog.

25

Scratches and Cuts

Minor skin irritations, such as scratches, can usually be cured by using an over-the-counter antibiotic cream or ointment. For minor skin problems, many ointments suitable for a baby work well on a Dachshund.

Heatstroke

Heatstroke can quickly lead to death. *Never* leave your dog in a car, even with the windows open, even on a

Make a temporary splint by wrapping the leg in firm casing, then bandaging it.

WHEN TO CALL THE VETERINARIAN

In any emergency situation, you should call your veterinarian immediately. Try to stay calm when you call, and give the vet or the assistant as much information as possible before you leave for the clinic. That way, the staff will be able to take immediate, specific action when you arrive. Emergencies include:

- Bleeding or deep wounds
- Hyperthermia (overheating)
- Shock
- Dehydration
- Abdominal pain
- Burns
- Fits
- Unconsciousness
- Broken bones
- Paralysis

Call your veterinarian if you suspect any health troubles.

cloudy day with the car under the shade of a tree. Heat builds up quickly; your dog could die in a matter of minutes. Do not leave your Dachshund outside on a hot day especially if no shade or water is provided.

Heatstroke symptoms include collapse, high fever, diarrhea, vomiting, excessive panting and grayish lips. If you notice these symptoms, you need to cool the animal immediately. Try to reduce the body temperature with towels soaked in cold water; massage the body and legs very gently. Fanning the dog may help. If the dog will drink cool water, let him. If he will not drink, wipe the inside of his mouth with cool water. Get the dog to the nearest veterinary hospital. Do not delay!

Bee Stings

Bee stings are painful and may cause an allergic reaction. Symptoms may be swelling around the bite and difficulty breathing. Severe allergic reaction could lead to death. If a stinger is present, remove it. Clean the bitten area thoroughly with alcohol; apply a cold compress to reduce swelling and itching and an anti-inflammatory ointment or cream medication. Seek medical help.

Choking

Puppies are curious creatures and will naturally chew anything they can get into their mouths, be it a bone, a twig, stones, tiny toys, string or any number of things. These can get caught in the teeth or, worse, lodged in the throat and may finally rest in the stomach or intestines. Symptoms may be drooling, pawing at the mouth, gagging, difficulty breathing, blue tongue or mouth, difficulty swallowing and bloody vomit. If the foreign object can be seen and you can remove it easily, do so. If you can't remove it yourself, use the Heimlich maneuver. Place your dog on his side and, using both hands palms down, apply quick thrusts to the abdomen, just below the dog's last rib. If your dog won't lie down, grasp either side of the end of the rib cage and squeeze in short thrusts. Make a sharp enough movement to cause the air in the lungs to force the object out. If the cause cannot be found or removed, then professional help is needed.

Bleeding

For open wounds, try to stop the bleeding by applying pressure to the wound for five minutes using a

Applying abdominal thrusts can save a choking dog.

sterile bandage. If bleeding has not stopped after this time, continue the pressure. Do not remove the pad if it sticks to the wound because more serious injury could result. Just place a new sterile bandage over the first, and apply a little more pressure to stop the bleeding. This procedure will usually be successful. Take the dog to the medical center for treatment especially if the bleeding cannot be controlled rapidly.

If bleeding cannot be stopped with pressure, try pressing on the upper inside of the front leg for bleeding of that limb; for the rear limbs, press on the upper inside of the rear leg; for tail bleeding, press on the underside of the tail at its base. Do not attempt to stop the bleeding with a tourniquet unless the bleeding is profuse and cannot be stopped any other way. A tourniquet must be tight; consequently, it cannot be left on for a long time because it will stop the circulation. It could be more dangerous than the bleeding!

27

As Dachshunds age, they are prone to cataracts and vision loss.

Burns

Do not put creams or oils on a burn. Cool water can be used to carefully wash the burn area. Transport to the veterinary clinic immediately.

COMMON DACHSHUND PROBLEMS

IMPACTED ANAL GLANDS—Anal glands are sacs located on each side of the rectum. If the sacs become impacted, your dog will be constantly preoccupied with his rear (licking, rubbing himself along the floor, rug or grass) and his rear will emit an unpleasant odor. Have him checked by a veterinarian as soon as possible.

CATARACTS (CLOUDED EYES)—If your dog is approaching his senior years, cataracts and loss of vision may naturally occur. Usually this requires no treatment, just clearing obstacles that might cause him harm. If this condition is noticed in a young dog, seek veterinary care.

CYSTS—Many older dogs develop cysts. Should you notice or feel a cyst with your hands when grooming or petting your dog, have your veterinarian check it. He will then advise you as to whether it should be watched (to see if it grows any larger) or if it should be biopsied.

DISC DISEASE—Disc disease is hereditary and usually manifests itself when the dog is between 2 to 5 years of age. Dachshunds with disc problems typically lose the use of their front and/or back legs. Depending on the severity of the condition, loss of mobility may only be temporary.

Disc problems range from minor to severe and often require only rest and medication. For the most severe cases, surgery may be recommended. However, many dogs have recovered quite well with acupuncture treatments and/or chiropractic adjustments.

They may have to go for a series of treatments over a period of years, but they can lead a life of dignity and be relatively pain free and moderately active.

DRY COAT—Evidenced by itching; dander visible to the eye; lackluster appearance. Dry coat is more prevalent in the winter when the heat is on and the humidity is low. Compensate for this by adding cod liver oil to the diet once or twice a week. Any oil, including vitamin E (break capsule and add to meal), will help.

EAR MITES—Once called "canker," ear mites are invisible to the naked eye and are contagious to other animals. Look for constant pulling at or scratching of ears; redness in ears; visible debris, usually black.

Seek veterinary attention if you believe your dog has ear mites.

LAMENESS—Symptoms include limping, not putting a foot down and favoring one paw. Before you do anything, check your dog's paw or paws. Make sure you check between his toes. There may be burrs or pieces of pinecones, which are sticky and get lodged in paws, pads of feet and between toes. Carefully remove those with the tweezers. If there is a cut and it is not bleeding profusely, apply

pressure until the bleeding stops, then put the foot on a gauze pad to fit. Wrap the pad with rolled gauze and secure with a gauze knot, not too tight. If you know from the start that it looks bad and the bleeding is profuse, go immediately to your veterinarian.

URINARY TRACT INFECTIONS—The Dachshund is low to the ground; thus females in particular can sometimes pick up urinary infections. Males can get them from licking, which causes pus to form in the sheath. Excess licking could be because of a urinary tract infection. Symptoms include excessive urination; attempts to urinate that produce small amounts of urine or nothing and blood in the urine. A urine sample should be taken to the veterinarian.

TAKING YOUR DACHSHUND'S TEMPERATURE

Learn to take your pet's temperature. An elevated or depressed temperature may spell the difference between your hound just being "off his feed" for a day or the presence of some infection, which could be best treated early.

WHAT'S WRONG WITH MY DOG?

We've listed some common conditions of health problems and their possible causes. If any of the following conditions appear serious or persist for more than 24 hours, make an appointment to see your veterinarian immediately.

CONDITIONS	POSSIBLE CAUSES
DIARRHEA	Intestinal upset, typically caused by eating something bad or over-eating. Can also be a viral infection, a bad case of nerves or anxiety or a parasite infection. If you see blood in the feces, get to the vet right away.
VOMITING/RETCHING	Dogs regurgitate fairly regularly (bitches for their young), whenever something upsets their stomachs, or even out of excitement or anxiety. Often dogs eat grass, which, because it's indigestible in its pure form, irritates their stomachs and causes them to vomit. Getting a good look at *what* your dog vomited can better indicate what's causing it.
COUGHING	Obstruction in the throat; virus (kennel cough); roundworm infestation; congestive heart failure.
RUNNY NOSE	Because dogs don't catch colds like people, a runny nose is a sign of congestion or irritation.
LOSS OF APPETITE	Because most dogs are hearty and regular eaters, a loss of appetite can be your first and most accurate sign of a serious problem.
LOSS OF ENERGY (LETHARGY)	Any number of things could be slowing down your dog, from an infection to internal tumors to overexercise—even overeating.

Ask someone to restrain the front end of your hound while you focus your attention on the other end. Grasp the base of the tail firmly, and with the other hand carefully insert a well-lubricated (with petroleum jelly) rectal thermometer into the anus. Holding your pet in this fashion should keep him fairly well immobilized.

CONDITIONS	POSSIBLE CAUSES
STINKY BREATH	Imagine if you never brushed your teeth! Foul-smelling breath indicates plaque and tartar buildup that could possibly have caused infection. Start brushing your dog's teeth.
LIMPING	This could be caused by something as simple as a hurt or bruised pad, to something as complicated as hip dysplasia, torn ligaments or broken bones.
CONSTANT ITCHING	Probably due to fleas, mites or an allergic reaction to food or environment (your vet will need to help you determine what your dog's allergic to).
RED, INFLAMED, ITCHY SPOTS	Often referred to as "hot spots," these are particularly common on coated breeds. They're caused by a bacterial infection that gets aggravated as the dog licks and bites at the spot.
BALD SPOTS	These are the result of excessive itching or biting at the skin so that the hair follicles are damaged; excessively dry skin; mange; calluses; and even infections. You need to determine what the underlying cause is.
STINKY EARS/HEAD SHAKING	Take a look under your dog's ear flap. Do you see brown, waxy buildup? Clean the ears with something soft and a special cleaner, and don't use cotton swabs or go too deep into the ear canal.
UNUSUAL LUMPS	Could be fatty tissue, could be something serious (infection, trauma, tumor). Don't wait to find out.

31

Be sure the thermometer you use is strong enough for this purpose; human oral-type thermometers are too fragile. The average temperature of the dog is approximately 101°F, but there may be normal variation of a degree or so either way, so taking your pet's temperature before he is sick is a good way of establishing what his "baseline" is.

PREVENTIVE CARE PAYS

Using common sense, paying attention to your dog and working with your veterinarian, you can minimize health risks and problems. Use vet-recommended flea, tick and heartworm preventive medications; feed a nutritious diet appropriate for your dog's size, age and activity level; give your dog sufficient exercise and regular grooming; train and socialize your dog; keep current on your dog's shots; and enjoy all the years you have with your friend.

MEDICATING YOUR DACHSHUND

If your vet sends you home with medication for your pet for whatever reason, have him or her demonstrate how to administer it.

If you have to give your hound a pill, put him on a table to get him closer to your eye level and immobilize him somewhat. With one hand, grasp the upper part of the muzzle and open his mouth. If you intentionally put his lips between his teeth and your fingers, he will be more reluctant to close his mouth before you are ready. With your other hand, place the pill as far back on his tongue as possible, taking care not to let it fall off to the side, where it may be bitten or expelled rather than swallowed. Close his mouth and hold his muzzle upright while stroking his throat to encourage swallowing. Keep doing this until you are sure he has swallowed. If your pet spits the pill out, keep at it until you succeed. You have to get the point across that you don't enjoy this any more than he does, but it has to be done!

Liquid medications are pretty rare these days, and if you can't add it to the feed, ask your vet for a syringe (minus the needle). This is a much more controlled method of administering liquids than spoons, but the principle is the same. Here you want to keep his mouth closed, only opening the lips at the corner of his mouth. You then inject or pour the liquid in as you tilt the head back slightly. And you keep the muzzle closed until he swallows.

CHAPTER FOUR

Positively Nutritious

T he nutritional needs of a dog will change throughout her lifetime. It is necessary to be aware of these changes not only for proper initial growth to occur, but also so your dog can lead a healthy life for many years.

Before bringing your puppy home, ask the breeder for the puppy's feeding schedule and information about what and how much she is used to eating. Maintain this regimen for at least the first few days before gradually changing to a schedule that is more in line with the family's lifestyle. The breeder may supply you with a small quantity of the food the puppy has been eating. Use this or have your own supply of the same food ready when you bring home your puppy.

After the puppy has been with you for three days and has become acclimated to her new environment, you can begin a gradual food change. Add a portion of the new food to the usual food. Add progressively more new food each day until it has entirely replaced the previous diet. This gradual change will prevent an upset stomach and diarrhea. The total amount of food to be fed at each meal will remain the same at this stage of the puppy's life.

LIFE-STAGE FEEDING

Puppies and adolescent dogs require a much higher intake of protein, calories and nutrients than adult dogs due to the demands of their rapidly developing bodies. Most commercial brands of dry kibble meet these requirements and are well balanced for proper growth. The majority of puppy foods now available are so carefully planned that it is unwise to attempt to add anything other than water to them.

Puppies and adolescent dogs require a high intake of protein, calories and nutrients to fuel their rapidly developing bodies.

The major ingredients of most dry dog foods are chicken, beef or lamb by-products and corn, wheat or rice. The higher the meat content, the higher the protein percentage, palatability and digestibility of the food. Protein requirements for puppies are much higher than those for adult dogs. There are many advantages of dry foods over semi-moist and canned dog foods for puppies and normal, healthy adult Dachshunds.

It is best to feed meals that are primarily dry food because the chewing action involved in eating a dry food is better for the health of the teeth and gums. Dry food is also less expensive than canned food of equal quality.

Dogs whose diets are based on canned or soft foods have a greater likelihood of developing calcium deposits and gum disease. Canned or semi-moist foods do serve certain functions, however. As a supplement to dry dog food, in small portions, canned or semi-moist foods can be useful to stimulate appetites and aid in weight gain. But unless very special conditions exist, they are not the best way for a dog to meet her food needs.

GROWTH STAGE FOODS

Once upon a time, there was puppy food and there was adult dog food. Now there are foods for puppies, young adults/active dogs, less active dogs and senior citizens. What's the difference between these foods? They vary by the amounts of nutrients they provide for the dog's growth stage/activity level.

Less active dogs don't need as much protein or fat as growing, active dogs; senior dogs don't need some of the nutrients vital to puppies. By feeding a high-quality food that's appropriate for your dog's age and activity level, you're benefiting your dog and yourself. Feed too much protein to a couch potato and she'll have energy to spare, which means a few more trips around the block will be needed to burn it off. Feed an adult diet to a puppy, and risk growth and development abnormalities that could affect her for a lifetime.

A FEEDING SCHEDULE

By the time you bring your puppy home, she will probably be at the stage where three meals will suffice. She should be fed morning, midday and evening. Fresh water should be available to her at all times. A good

FOOD ALLERGIES

If your puppy or dog seems to itch all the time for no apparent reason, she could be allergic to one or more ingredients in her food. This is not uncommon, and it's why many foods contain lamb and rice instead of beef, wheat or soy. Have your dog tested by your veterinarian, and be patient while you strive to identify and eliminate the allergens from your dog's food (or environment).

This is something that can only be accomplished by observation and good judgment.

plan to follow is to divide the amount recommended by the veterinarian by three. If the puppy is finishing all three of these portions throughout the day and the appearance of the body indicates proper growth, then stay with those amounts. If the puppy looks like she is gaining weight excessively, then reduce the amount that is given. The same applies for the puppy that leaves quantities of food uneaten, yet is at a good weight and energy level otherwise. Obviously, if a puppy is eating her rations and appears thin, her food intake should be increased.

Feeding your Dachshund dry food helps keep her teeth and gums healthy.

From 6 months to 1 year of age, the puppy should remain on puppy food, but the feedings should decrease to twice a day. By the time a dog reaches 1 year of age, she should be switched to an adult maintenance diet. The number of feedings can remain at twice a day, though it is easier for most owners to feed a large meal once a day.

Puppies and dogs should have a place of their own where they can eat their meals without disturbance. A dog's crate can be an ideal place to feed a dog. Give a dog a definite period of time to eat her food rather than allowing her to nibble throughout the day. If the food has not been eaten within a ten-minute period, pick it up and do not feed again until the next mealtime. One of the best ways to spot health problems in dogs, and Dachshunds in particular because they tend to be good eaters, is monitoring their food intake. Most Dachshunds that miss more than one meal under normal circumstances are not well.

Some owners like to add variety to their dogs' lives with human food. Scraps given regularly can lead to weight gain if the amount of the dog's regular food is not reduced. The risk of destroying the

Your dog may let you know when it's her mealtime.

HOW MANY MEALS A DAY?

Individual dogs vary in how much they should eat to maintain a desired body weight—not too fat, but not too thin. Puppies need several meals a day, while older dogs may need only one. Determine how much food keeps your adult dog looking and feeling her best. Then decide how many meals you want to feed with that amount. Like us, most dogs love to eat, and offering two meals a day is more enjoyable for them. If you're worried about overfeeding, make sure you measure correctly and abstain from adding tidbits to the meals.

Whether you feed one or two meals, only leave your dog's food out for the amount of time it takes her to eat it—ten minutes, for example. Free-feeding (when food is available any time) and leisurely meals encourage picky eating. Don't worry if your dog doesn't finish all her dinner in the allotted time. She'll learn she should.

37

Fresh, clean water should be available to your Dachshund at all times.

TO SUPPLEMENT OR NOT TO SUPPLEMENT?

If you're feeding your dog a diet that's correct for her developmental stage and she's alert, healthy looking and neither over- nor underweight, you don't need to add supplements. These include table scraps as well as vitamins and minerals. In fact, unless you are a nutrition expert, using food supplements can actually hurt a growing puppy. For example, mixing too much calcium into your dog's food can lead to musculoskeletal disorders. Educating yourself about the quantity of vitamins and minerals your dog needs to be healthy will help you determine what needs to be supplemented. If you have any concerns about the nutritional quality of the food you're feeding, discuss them with your veterinarian.

nutritional balance of the dog food also exists. Some human foods fed in large quantities can lead to gastrointestinal problems, which can result in loose stools and even diarrhea.

The amount of food an adult Dachshund should eat daily will vary according to the size of the dog, her activity level and how much time she spends outside.

Most Dachshund owners should consider placing their dog on a food that is very low in fat and protein content by the age of 8 or 9, unless the dog is still very active. A dog that is inactive, either by choice or the owner's laziness, has lower nutritional requirements. Another thing to keep in mind is that as dogs age, their kidneys can be destroyed if kept on a food with high protein content. Foods formulated for older dogs are low in fat and protein content.

Maintaining the proper weight and nutrition of an older Dachshund is probably more difficult than at any other stage of life. A certain amount of body fat is necessary to protect her in the event of illness. Too much excess weight will make the dog even less active and more prone to physical problems. If a dog develops such problems as kidney failure, heart disease or an overly sensitive digestive tract, there are specially formulated foods commercially available.

Older Dachshunds may need a special diet to keep them at their optimum weight.

HOW TO READ THE DOG FOOD LABEL

With so many choices on the market, how can you be sure you are feeding the right food to your dog? The information is all there on the label—if you know what you're looking for.

Look for the nutritional claim right up top. Is the food "100 percent nutritionally complete"? If so, it's for nearly all life stages; "growth and maintenance," on the other hand, is for early development; puppy foods are marked as such, as are foods for senior dogs.

Ingredients are listed in descending order by weight. The first three or four ingredients will tell you the bulk of what the food contains. Look for the highest-quality ingredients, like meats and grains, to be among them.

The Guaranteed Analysis tells you what levels of protein, fat, fiber and moisture are in the food, in that order. While these numbers are meaningful, they won't tell you much about the quality of the food. Nutritional value is in the dry matter, not the moisture content.

In many ways, seeing is believing. If your dog has bright eyes, a shiny coat, a good appetite and a good energy level, chances are her diet's fine. Your dog's breeder and your veterinarian are good sources of advice if you're still confused.

The physical appearance a Dachshund presents is as much a result of genetics as it is the food she eats. The owner that feeds a high quality food and keeps her in optimum weight for her size will be rewarded with a Dachshund whose health and fitness mirrors her diet.

CHAPTER FIVE

Putting on the Dog

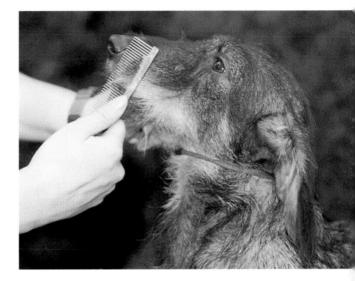

The Dachshund is a low-maintenance dog and can usually be groomed at home with relative ease. If properly fed and exercised, the breed presents a pleasing picture—compact, neat, conditioned and athletic. Therefore, you also want him to be clean and well groomed.

BASIC SUPPLIES

There are some general grooming supplies you will need for your Dachshund, regardless of the variety you own:

- bath mat
- shampoo and conditioner (specially formulated for dogs)
- rubbing alcohol
- soft-bristled toothbrush
- toothpaste (for dogs)
- canine nail clipper
- cotton balls
- flea comb
- ear-cleaning solution
- grooming table (optional)
- rubber mat (optional)

Unless your Dachshund comes into contact with some malodorous animal or rolls in something less than

GROOMING TOOLS

- pin brush
- slicker brush
- flea comb
- towel
- mat rake
- grooming glove
- scissors
- nail clippers
- tooth-cleaning equipment
- shampoo
- conditioner
- clippers

pleasant, frequent bathing is not necessary. It removes the natural oils from the skin and causes dander. Under normal conditions, once every few months should suffice. A good brushing session will do more to clean your dog's coat than soap and water.

GROOMING YOUR SMOOTH DACHSHUND

Aside from the basic grooming necessities, what you want for your smooth is a rubber brush, a hound glove/mitt or a natural-bristle brush (soft to medium). A comb is really not necessary for the smooth, nor are the scissors

if your dog is not being shown. In the show ring, the whiskers are cut to present a cleaner line, but your pet can keep his!

The more you stroke your smooth, the more you stimulate the natural oils of his skin, loosen the dead hair and keep the coat's shine. So, while your Dachshund is lying next to you on the floor or the sofa, you can kill two birds with one stone: Give him extra attention and groom him at the same time!

If you don't want to use your hand, the hound glove or mitt is a good alternative. It fits your hand like a mitt (hence the name) and has a nubby surface on the down side. Rubbing this along the smooth coat will banish the loose hair and stimulate the natural oils.

If you do this a little each day, your Dachshund won't even realize he's being groomed and will sleep through the whole procedure—especially if you begin when he's a young puppy.

GROOMING YOUR LONGHAIRED DACHSHUND

You'll need more grooming equipment for the longhair:

42

- a pin brush

- blunt-edged (rounded) scissors

- tangle remover

- a fine- to medium-toothed comb

The longhaired coat needs more aggressive and frequent grooming than the smooth. If you don't work on his coat at least every other day, it will mat and tangle and your task will be unpleasant for your dog and a chore for you!

The pin brush is an efficient tool for this type of coat. It will go deep into the undercoat as well as the surface and help prevent tangling.

If you don't have a grooming table, use the floor. Have the dog lie on his side, (a female needs to stand) and before you begin to brush, use your fingers to feel for mats or tangles, especially in the armpit area and in the feathering on the legs. There are products on the market that, when soaked into the tangles, will soften them so you can work them gently with your fingers. Please remember that combing tangles out before undoing them will cause your dog a great deal of discomfort.

Once you have brushed and combed out both sides and the feathering on all four legs, you'll need to deal with the tail and with his feet.

Taking the blunt-edged scissors, you need to trim around the edges of each foot and also between the toes. Then, holding his tail straight

A healthy, well-groomed Dachs-hund makes a pleasing picture.

The more you brush your smooth Dachshund, the more his coat will shine.

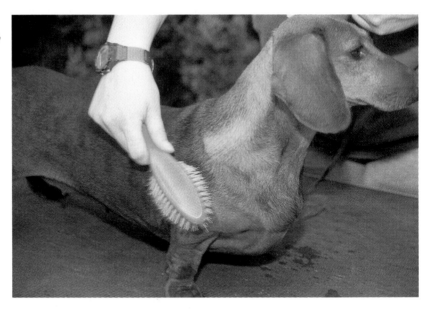

44

You will need a pin brush to groom your longhaired Dachshund.

out from the base, you need to trim the underside of the tail so he won't soil himself when he defecates. Using the blunt-edged scissors, keep the tail extended with one hand and scissor with the other from the base out about an inch or more.

If you find these tasks unpleasant or are afraid you will harm your dog, have a professional groomer do them. Obviously, the dog must be kept still when you scissor these areas, and the female needs to be standing.

When you use the brush or the comb on your longhair, go in the natural direction of the hair. You want the coat flat, not curled or wavy.

GROOMING YOUR WIREHAIRED DACHSHUND

And finally, the wire coat. You'll need:

- a stripping comb
- blunt-edged scissors
- a pin brush
- a medium-toothed comb
- a hound glove
- thinning scissors

Just how tight your dog's coat is will determine what tools you'll need to use. A really rough- or tight-coated wire needs, like the smooth, minimal care. A stripping comb (never a razor-edged comb) is used gently down the back on a slant, to thin out the guard hairs. Never dig into the coat but skim on the angle. You're thinning, not cutting. How often do you need to do this? You'll know when you see the hair sticking up a little along his back, looking rather unkempt.

You can run a comb through his beard as often as needed to keep it from tangling, and you can use the thinning shears if the beard or eyebrows are too long or too thick. When you use the thinning shears, use short, quick motions. When you draw them away from the dog's

beard, do it gently or you will pull hair and cause your dog some discomfort. (The blades on the thinning shears should be in the open position, which will allow you to remove the shears easily.) It will also be necessary to trim the hairs around the genital area and around the vulva so they don't tangle if they become long enough. That will also depend on how tight the coat is. The rest of the coat can be brushed with the pin brush or the hound mitt.

The soft-coated wire should be taken down with the clippers by a professional groomer or a Dachshund breeder. The soft coat is fine and often long and will mat and tangle. It will require much daily maintenance and will be quite time-consuming. A coat like this should be clipped several times a year, depending on the dog. Having it clipped during the summer months helps keep fleas and ticks under control.

GROOMING REGARDLESS OF COAT TYPE

Now to the grooming, which must be done regardless of the coat variety of your Dachshund. Routinely check your dog's ears—at least once a

45

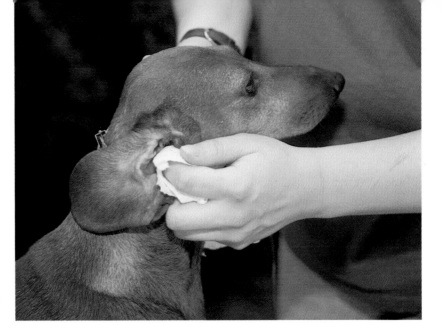

Check and clean your dog's ears at least once a week.

week. Take a cotton ball dipped in alcohol and gently rub it around the inside of the ear. You also need to use an ear solution to loosen the wax buildup. Put a few drops into the inner ear and then gently rub the base of the outer ear between your thumb and index finger. This will help to loosen any wax; then you can take some cotton or a tissue, wrap it around your finger and gently remove the loosened wax.

You must clip your dog's nails regularly. Begin cutting your puppy's nails early on—hold him on your lap and play with his feet. Handle them, stroke them, get him accustomed to having them touched. Make sure you praise him often.

Also, rub the nail clippers across his paws. Let him smell them, and feel them, all the while telling him they won't hurt him. Speak to him in soothing tones and gently take hold of his paw and barely tip the nail. Go slowly and stop before he starts to object. During each session, give him several treats.

You need only cut the tips of the nails off. It is difficult to see the quick on the Dachshund's nail. But if you misjudge and the nail bleeds, use a styptic powder to stop it. Place the powder on the nail, applying gentle pressure.

If you can't manage the nails yourself, have your veterinarian clip them. Nails that are too long throw the dog off balance and may cause back problems. Also, if the nail is too long, it will eventually turn inward, which makes it difficult to cut because of the proximity to the pad. If that is the case, let your veterinarian do it.

As far as bathing goes, when you do it, make sure that the dog has proper footing. And when you're finished, make sure your Dachshund can't get outside since, when freed, he will roll over and scratch his back!

Place cotton in his ears to prevent them from becoming waterlogged. With warm, never hot, water, using a hose attachment, soak his coat. Then lather him with whatever shampoo you want to use, starting from the base of the tail up toward the head. On the head, switch to a tear-free shampoo, if you're not already using one, to protect his eyes. When you've rubbed the soap gently through the coat, rinse him well! With the longs and the smooths, you may want to use a conditioner or creme rinse, but do not do so with the tight-coated wire. You do not want a soft coat here.

When you are sure the soap is well rinsed out, towel dry your smooth briskly; your wire, with strokes going flat so as not to ruffle; your long, with the towel draped to keep the coat

QUICK AND PAINLESS NAIL CLIPPING

This is possible if you make a habit out of handling your dog's feet and giving your dog treats when you do. When it's time to clip nails, go through the same routine, but take your clippers and snip off just the ends of the nail—clip too far down and you'll cut into the "quick," the nerve center, hurting your dog and causing the nail to bleed. Clip two nails a session while you're getting your dog used to the procedure, and you'll soon be doing all four feet quickly and easily.

flat. You may use the blow-dryer on all coats if the dog is not afraid. If you choose to do so with the longhair, brush the coat by pulling it away and then letting it fall flat against his side. You don't want the longhair to be fuzzy or curly. His fur should stay flat on the body, like that of an Irish Setter.

If you begin early, your dog will accept the blow-dryer. Be sure to dry the feet and between the toes of the smooth, particularly.

CARING FOR TEETH

We rarely think about the cleanliness of our dogs' teeth, leaving that to the

47

Don't forget to clean your Dachshund's teeth regularly.

natural cleansing action of chewing. However, dogs develop gum disease and tooth degeneration just like humans. We can help counter this progression by brushing the teeth regularly. Canine toothpastes and toothbrushes are available and can be used daily.

CHAPTER SIX

Measuring Up

THE OFFICIAL STANDARD FOR THE DACHSHUND

The following is the standard approved by the American Kennel Club in 1992.

General Appearance

Low to ground, long in body and short of leg with robust muscular development, the skin is elastic and pliable without excessive wrinkling.

Appearing neither crippled, awkward, nor cramped in his capacity for movement, the Dachshund is well-balanced with bold and confident head carriage and intelligent, alert facial expression. His hunting spirit, good nose, loud tongue and distinctive build make him well-suited for below-ground work and

WHAT IS A BREED STANDARD?

A breed standard—a detailed description of an individual breed—is meant to portray the ideal specimen of that breed. This includes ideal structure, temperament, gait, type—all aspects of the dog. Because the standard describes an ideal specimen, it isn't based on any particular dog. It is a concept against which judges compare actual dogs and breeders strive to produce dogs. At a dog show, the dog that wins is the one that comes closest, in the judge's opinion, to the standard for its breed. Breed standards are written by the breed parent clubs, the national organizations formed to oversee the well-being of the breed. They are voted on and approved by the members of the parent clubs.

for beating the bush. His keen nose gives him an advantage over most other breeds for trailing. NOTE: Inasmuch as the Dachshund is a hunting dog, scars from honorable wounds shall not be considered a fault.

Size, Proportion, Substance

Bred and shown in two sizes, standard and miniature. Miniatures are not a separate classification but compete in a class division for "11 pounds and under at 12 months of age and older." Weight of the standard size is usually between 16 and 32 pounds.

While there is no absolute limit for the Standard, the Dachshund Club of America suggests that she range from 16 to 32 pounds. The Miniature, on the other hand, is carefully monitored. At 12 months of age, she must be 11 pounds or under—and should remain so. Other than the weight classification, there is no difference between the two sizes. The purpose of the dog and the standard by which she is judged are the same.

Head

Viewed from above or from the side, the head tapers uniformly to the tip of the nose. The **eyes** are of medium size, almond-shaped and dark-rimmed, with an energetic, pleasant expression; not piercing; very dark in color. The bridge bones over the eyes are strongly prominent. Wall eyes, except in the case of dappled dogs, are a serious fault. The **ears** are set near the top of the head, not too far forward, of moderate length, rounded, not narrow, pointed, or folded. Their carriage, when animated, is with the forward edge just touching the cheek so that the ears frame the face. The **skull** is slightly arched, neither too

*broad nor too narrow, and slopes grad-
ually with little perceptible stop into the
finely-formed, slightly arched muzzle.
Black is the preferred color of the nose.
Lips are tightly stretched, well covering
the lower jaw. Nostrils well open. Jaws
opening wide and hinged well back of
the eyes, with strongly developed bones
and teeth. **Teeth**—Powerful canine
teeth; teeth fit closely together in a scissors bite. An even bite is a minor fault.
Any other deviation is a serious fault.*

The Dachshund is a scent hunter,
and when she hunts, she is a formi-
dable foe. Her jaws and teeth are
strong and powerful. Her nose, with
the help of her length of ear, picks
up the scent and she is off on her
mission. If she did not "give tongue"
as she worked, the hunters would be
hard-pressed to follow, as the Dachshund does not travel in a straight
line when tracking and once gone to
ground, locating her would indeed be

THE AMERICAN KENNEL CLUB

Familiarly referred to as "the AKC," the American Kennel Club is a nonprofit organization
devoted to the advancement of purebred dogs.
The AKC maintains a registry of recognized
breeds and adopts and enforces rules for dog
events including shows, obedience trials, field
trials, hunting tests, lure coursing, herding,
earthdog trials, agility and the Canine Good
Citizen program. It is a club of clubs, established
in 1884 and composed, today, of over 500
autonomous dog clubs throughout the United
States. Each club is represented by a delegate;
the delegates make up the legislative body of
the AKC, voting on rules and electing directors.
The American Kennel Club maintains the Stud
Book, the record of every dog ever registered with
the AKC, and publishes a variety of materials on
purebred dogs, including a monthly magazine,
books and numerous educational pamphlets. For
more information, contact the AKC at the
address listed in Chapter 9, "Resources."

51

*Dachshunds
should have an
intelligent, alert
facial expression.*

The miniature Dachshund should weigh no more than 11 pounds.

a challenge if not for the melodious tonguing of a dog who has cornered her prey.

Neck

Long, muscular, clean-cut, without dewlap, slightly arched in the nape, flowing gracefully into the shoulders.

Trunk

The trunk is long and fully muscled. When viewed in profile, the back lies in the straightest possible line between the withers and the short very slightly arched loin. A body that hangs loosely between the shoulders is a serious fault. **Abdomen**—*Slightly drawn up.*

Forequarters

For effective underground work, the front must be strong, deep, long and cleanly muscled. Forequarters in detail:

Chest—*The breastbone is strongly prominent in front so that on either side a depression or dimple appears. When viewed from the front, the thorax appears oval and extends downward to the mid-point of the forearm. The enclosing structure of well-sprung ribs appears full and oval to allow, by its ample capacity, complete development of heart and lungs. The keel merges gradually into the line of the abdomen and extends well beyond the front legs. Viewed in profile, the lowest point of the breast line is covered by the front leg.* **Shoulder Blades**—*Long, broad, well-laid back and firmly placed upon the fully developed thorax, closely fitted at the withers, furnished with hard yet pliable muscles.* **Upper Arm**—*Ideally the same length as the shoulder blade and at right angles to the latter, strong of bone and hard of muscle, lying close to the ribs, with elbows close to the body, yet capable of free movement.* **Forearm**—*Short; supplied with hard yet pliable muscles on the front and outside, with tightly stretched tendons on the inside and at the back, slightly curved inwards. The joints between the forearms and the feet (wrists) are closer together than the shoulder joints, so that the front does not appear absolutely straight. Knuckling over is a disqualifying fault.* **Feet**—*Front paws are full,* *tight, compact, with well-arched toes and tough, thick pads. They may be equally inclined a trifle outward. There are five toes, four in use, close together with a pronounced arch and strong, short nails. Front dewclaws may be removed.*

The ideal Dachshund must be well-balanced. And one of the most important aspects of the standard is the neck and forequarters. A short neck directly affects the shoulder placement, and poor angulation in the neck does not allow the dog proper reach when moving forward. In the hunting Dachshund, we need stamina over speed. Short-legged hounds hunt with endurance. Therefore, the Dachshund hock must be strong. If these aspects of the hunting hound are not as correct as they should be, it hampers the performance and the stamina and thus may cause injury to the dog in the field.

This dog must have the capacity to breathe underground and the muscular agility that enables her to maneuver the earth when she goes to ground. She needs to be low enough to slide into the earth and yet have enough leg under her to prevent injury to herself. Her hindquarters must be strong enough to propel her forward and to keep her keel and powerful forechest from scraping the ground. It is the balance of the forechest, brisket and hocks working together, along with the elasticity of her muscles, that enables this hound to move with ease through the maze of underground tunnels. She must be muscular, with no skin loose enough to allow her prey to grab hold, which is why the standard states that there should be no wrinkles or dewlap.

Hindquarters

Strong and cleanly muscled. The pelvis, the thigh, the second thigh, and the metatarsus are ideally the same length and form a series of right angles. From the rear, the thighs are strong and powerful. The legs turn neither in nor out. **Metatarsus**—*short and strong, perpendicular to the second thigh bone. When viewed from behind, they are upright and parallel.* **Feet**—*Hind Paws—Smaller than the front paws with four compactly closed and arched toes with tough, thick pads. The entire foot points straight ahead and is balanced equally on the ball and not merely on the toes. Rear dewclaws should be removed.* **Croup**—*Long, rounded and full, sinking slightly toward the tail.*

The Dachshund should be well-balanced and muscular.

Tail—*Set in continuation of the spine, extending without kinks, twists, or pronounced curvature, and not carried too gaily.*

Gait

Fluid and smooth. Forelegs reach well forward, without much lift, in unison with the driving action of the hind legs. The correct shoulder assembly and well fitted elbows allow the long, free stride in front. Viewed from the front, the legs do not move in exact parallel planes, but incline slightly inward to compensate for shortness of leg and width of chest. Hind legs drive on a line with the forelegs, with hocks (metatarsus) turning neither in nor out. The propulsion of the hind leg depends on the dog's ability to carry the hind leg to complete extension. Viewed in profile, the forward reach of the hind leg equals the rear extension. The thrust of correct movement is seen when the rear pads are clearly exposed during rear extension. Feet must travel parallel to the line of motion with no tendency to swing out, cross over, or interfere with each other. Short, choppy movement, rolling or high-stepping gait, close or overly wide coming or going are incorrect. The Dachshund must have agility, freedom of movement, and endurance to do the work for which he was developed.

When the Dachshund moves, her gait should be "fluid and smooth."

Her forelegs should "reach well forward without much lift." Simply put, she should not paddle the air or prance. Such movements are wasted energy for a dog bred for stamina.

The Dachshund must be agile and have the endurance to do hunting for which the breed was developed. The Miniature carries bone and substance appropriate for her weight, and since the Dachshund is a dog of substance and stamina, both sizes should possess "robust muscular development." The words "strong," "powerful" and "muscular" appear quite often in the standard for a reason!

Temperament

The Dachshund is clever, lively and courageous to the point of rashness, persevering in above and below ground work, with all the senses well-developed. Any display of shyness is a serious fault.

A dog raised in the proper environment should come to you willingly, with tail wagging. She will also not come to you, with tail wagging, just as well! Her sense of comic fun will often lead you on a merry chase, and her agility and speed will amaze you! She is, as the standard says, "clever" and "agile"!

She also perseveres! She is agile enough to squeeze out of any door or gate you try to close behind you should she feel she wants to come along. She is people-oriented and she is an extrovert. She will outsmart and outthink you any time the chance arises. She does not, at any time, consider herself a small dog.

Special Characteristics of the Three Coat Varieties

The Dachshund is bred with three varieties of coat: (1) smooth; (2) wirehaired; (3) longhaired and is shown in two sizes, standard and miniature. All three varieties and both sizes must conform to the characteristics already specified. The following features are applicable for each variety:

SMOOTH DACHSHUND

Coat—Short, smooth and shining. Should be neither too long nor too thick. Ears not leathery. Tail—Gradually tapered to a point, well but not too richly haired. Long sleek bristles on the underside are considered a patch of strong-growing hair, not a fault. A brush tail is a fault, as is a partly or wholly hairless tail. Color of Hair—Although base color is immaterial, certain patterns and basic colors predominate.

One-colored Dachshunds include red (with or without a shading of interspersed dark hairs or sable) and cream. A small amount of white on the chest is acceptable, but not desirable. **Nose and nails**—black. **Two-colored Dachshunds** include black, chocolate, wild boar, gray (blue) and fawn (Isabella), each with tan markings over the eyes, on the sides of the jaw and underlip, on the inner edge of the ear, front legs, on the paws and around the anus, and from there to about one-third to one-half of the length of the tail on the underside. Undue prominence or extreme lightness of tan markings is undesirable. **Nose and nails**—in the case of black dogs, black; for chocolate and all other colors, dark brown, but self-colored is acceptable. **Dappled Dachshunds**—The "single" dapple pattern is expressed as lighter-colored areas contrasting with the darker base color, which may be any acceptable color. Neither the light nor the dark color should predominate. **Nose and nails** are the same as for one- and two-colored Dachshunds. Partial or wholly blue (wall) eyes are as acceptable as dark eyes. A large area of white on the chest of a dapple is permissible.

Brindle is a pattern (as opposed to a color) in which black or dark stripes occur over the entire body although in some specimens the pattern may be visible only in the tan points.

WIREHAIRED DACHSHUND

Coat—With the exception of jaw, eyebrows, and ears, the whole body is covered with a uniform tight, short, thick, rough, hard outer coat but with finer, somewhat softer, shorter hairs

A longhaired, wirehaired and smooth Dachshund are lovingly cradled by their owner.

(undercoat) everywhere distributed between the coarser hairs. The absence of an undercoat is a fault. The distinctive facial furnishings include a beard and eyebrows. On the ears the hair is shorter than on the body, almost smooth. The general arrangement of the hair is such that the wirehaired Dachshund, when viewed from a distance, resembles the smooth. Any sort of soft hair in the outercoat, wherever found on the body, especially on the top of the head, is a fault. The same is true of long, curly, or wavy hair, or hair that sticks out irregularly in all directions. **Tail**—Robust, thickly haired, gradually tapering to a point. A flag tail is a fault. **Color of Hair**—While the most common colors are wild boar, black and tan, and various shades of red, all colors are admissible. A small amount of white on the chest, although acceptable, is not desirable. **Nose and nails**—same as for the smooth variety.

LONGHAIRED DACHSHUND

Coat—The sleek, glistening, often slightly wavy hair is longer under the neck and on forechest, the underside of the body, the ears, and behind the legs. The coat gives the dog an elegant appearance. Short hair on the ear is not desirable. Too profuse a coat which masks type, equally long hair over the whole body, a curly coat, or a pronounced parting on the back are faults. **Tail**—Carried gracefully in prolongation of the spine; the hair attains its greatest length here and forms a veritable flag. **Color of Hair**—Same as for the smooth Dachshund. **Nose and nails** same as for the smooth.

The foregoing description is that of the ideal Dachshund. Any deviation from the above described dog must be penalized to the extent of the deviation keeping in mind the importance of the contribution of the various features toward the basic original purpose of the breed.

Disqualification

Knuckling over of front legs.

There is no perfect Dachshund in the world; every dog has some fault or weakness. It is the *overall* appearance and attitude that are most important in evaluating the Dachshund. While faults might affect a dog is she were to be entered in a dog show, they will have no bearing on a dog's ability to be a good companion. Remember this when reading the standard and when applying it to your own dog.

CHAPTER SEVEN

A Matter of Fact

THE DACHSHUND'S ROOTS

It is commonly agreed that the Dachshund as we know him came out of Germany. John Hutchinson Cook, known until his death in 1994 as "Mr. Dachshund" by those in the dog world, and a noted breeder and judge, had done endless research on this breed, which was so close to his heart. He felt that the Dachshund might have come to Germany when the Hapsburg heir, Maximilian, journeyed from Vienna to wed the daughter of the Duke of Burgundy in 1477. His future father-in-law, Charles the Bold,

The early history of many of our purebred dogs is often woven through the legends and stories of several countries. The Dachshund is no exception. Some researchers think that a dog resembling this breed was pictured on Egyptian tombs, making the Dachshund more than 4,000 years old.

maintained hunting hounds by the thousands as well as extensive land holdings, since it is a well-known fact that in those times hunting and hunting hounds were pleasures afforded the wealthy nobles.

Some of these hounds, owned by Charles, the Duke of Burgundy, accompanied those who had journeyed with Maximilian when they returned home to Austria, where they were used to hunt in packs. Mr. Cook felt strongly that from those original Burgundy hounds, which were selectively bred down the centuries, the Dachshund evolved.

Whatever the theories one holds, the Dachshund as we know him today was developed and refined by the German foresters into what they needed—a fearless hunter with intelligence who could work above and below ground over various terrains, who was obstinate and rash enough to hold his prey at bay until the hunter could finish the deed.

NAMING THE DACHSHUND

It is a commonly accepted fact that the name Dachshund(e) is German

WHERE DID DOGS COME FROM?

It can be argued that dogs were right there at man's side from the beginning of time. As soon as human beings began to document their existence, the dog was among their drawings and inscriptions. Dogs were not just friends, they served a purpose: There were dogs to hunt birds, pull sleds, herd sheep, burrow after rats—even sit in laps! What your dog was originally bred to do influences the way he behaves. The American Kennel Club recognizes over 140 breeds, and there are hundreds more distinct breeds around the world. To make sense of the breeds, they are grouped according to their size or function. The AKC has seven groups:

1. Sporting
2. Working
3. Herding
4. Hounds
5. Terriers
6. Toys
7. Non Sporting

Can you name a breed from each group? Here's some help: (1) Golden Retriever; (2) Doberman Pinscher; (3) Collie; (4) Beagle; (5) Scottish Terrier; (6) Maltese; and (7) Dalmatian. All modern domestic dogs (*Canis familiaris*) are related, however different they look, and are all descended from *Canis lupus,* the gray wolf.

first German Stud Book and made the first list of desirable characteristics of the breed. In 1888, the Teckel Klub (Dachshund Club) was founded. It set up its own stud book and tried to work out some arrangement with the Delegate Commission, but that never materialized. As a result, the Dachshund fancy began to split, since some dogs were listed in the Teckel Klub Book and some in the one maintained by the Delegate Commission.

It is thought that Dachshunds were used as hunting hounds in Germany in the 1400s.

in origin and means "Badger Dog." Because the English presumed *hunde* meant "hound," the dog became a "Dachshund" minus the "e" instead of "Badger Dog" and ended up eventually in the Hound Group, though the breed was originally classified as a Working dog and then a Sporting dog by the AKC (though it was not used exclusively as a gun dog). The Dachshund does hunt on the scent like the Beagle and other scenthounds, but he also goes to earth and in that respect is an "earthdog" or "terrier."

The German revolution of 1848 put breeding dogs on the back burner, but the national foresters in all likelihood continued the practice because in 1879 Germany issued its

BECOMING POPULAR

Many local clubs formed all over Germany as the Dachshund began to increase in popularity. This gave rise to another so-called split. In 1895, many breeders began to concern themselves with producing dogs for the show ring and began to breed to that end. These dogs increased the breed's size and also the depth of chest. Some breeders felt such a goal was lessening the agility of the dog as a working hunter.

By 1895, the Dachshund came to be the largest entry of any breed in the dog shows. This caused some problems with breeders, some of whom allowed the dog's features to be exaggerated. Also, to be registered in the German Stud Book, any member of the Dachshund Club could make a decision as to whether a dog should be included. And most were, unless the animal was discovered to have faults that made him or her unsuitable for breeding.

Dr. Engelmann was one of those who was very instrumental in trying to change the new mentality, and in 1905 the "hunting dachshund" movement began.

In 1910, the German Hunting Dachshund Club was formed. Breeders split according to their interest, and the Delegate Commission tried to keep both groups happy. Failing to do so, the commission lost its leadership status. The German Hunting Dachshund Club later, in an unselfish gesture, dissolved itself in order to create the Federation of German Working Dachshund Clubs. It was this federation that set up the standard for working Dachshunds.

In 1905, a club for the Breeding of the Miniature Dachshund was formed, but after ten years of unsuccessfully trying to develop true Dachshund type that would consistently produce the small dog they desired, they disbanded. That same year,

The Dachshund is a scent hunter as well as an earthdog.

Forester Kroepelin had a kennel of small Dachshunds and formed a new club—The Miniature Dachshund Club.

At this point, each nationally organized club maintained and published its own stud book. The only one, however, who did more than simply register pedigrees was the Working Dachshund Club, which listed only those dogs that passed certain tests set up by the federation.

It is widely accepted that the smooth variety was first on the scene. According to Herman Cox, noted Dachshund breeder and judge, the first wirehair appeared in 1812, though he does mention in his book *Cox on Dachshunds* that "in 1836, some sixty years before the three varieties reached their popularity in Germany, Dr. Reichbach included in his discussion portraits of all three varieties."

The longhair appeared to be around in 1820 but did not reach the show ring until 1882, when a longhair owned by a Captain v. Brieman of Bernberg was shown. The captain had been breeding that variety since 1874, and when the standard for the longhair was written in 1882, it was the captain's dog that they used as a model.

In 1909, in order to bring all independent clubs together, one club, the Association of German Working Dachshund Clubs, was formed. This served to unify breeders, and they worked together until World War I.

England played a vital part in the Dachshund's history by writing the first standard of perfection for the breed. It was abandoned in 1907, however, when the English adopted the German standard, since over the years, the English breeders had developed great respect for the Dachshund coming out of Germany.

TWENTIETH-CENTURY HOUNDS

By the early 1900s, the Dachshund breeders of the years before finally were able to produce dogs that were relatively free of the major faults the breed had been plagued with up to that point. In 1911, 1912 and 1913, respectively, the lines that became the backbone of our present-day Dachshund evolved: The Flottenberg prefix, bred by G. F. Muller (1911); the Lindenbuhl prefix, bred by Simon Barthel (1912); and the Luilpoldsheim prefix, bred by Emil Sensenbienner (1913).

In the beginning, the Dachshund came to America in three ways—with the military who found the breed appealing and returned home with one in tow; with those wealthy enough to travel abroad and return with breeding and show stock; and with those who emigrated to America and promoted the breed.

One of those who imported excellent stock from Germany was a man by the name of Herbert Bertrands, who with his wife, Ellen, established the famous Ellenbert Kennels. The Flottenberg dogs appealed to them, so they imported stock from this German kennel regularly.

Herbert Sanborn also played an important role in those early years. Having studied in Germany in the early 1900s, he showed his dogs in Europe before he brought them to the United States and was able to continue their show careers and use them as breeding stock for his Isartal foundation dogs.

There were a few people, however, who were the backbone of the American breeding program, and they were also the guiding spirits of the Dachshund Club of America: Harry Peters Sr.; G. Muss-Arnolt, an artist; and Dr. Montebacher, a

doctor and chemist. Interestingly, Dr. Montebacher kenneled his dogs in his drugstore, under the shelves! When he died, his dogs went to Mr. Peters, and since Dr. Montebacher was interested in dapple Dachshunds, when Mr. Peters took over his dogs, he had among them some of the "tiger" Dachshunds, as they were then known. It was Mr. Peters Sr., who was therefore to make history by showing the first dapple Dachshunds in this country. It was also Mr. Peters Sr. who became the first president of the Dachshund Club of America.

The person, however, whom many credit with holding the breed and the Dachshund Club of America together, and who continued to operate her kennel during those trying years of WWI, was Mrs. C. Davies Tainter of Voewood fame.

The AKC remained firm in its stand that they did not want six Dachshunds in the Hound Group, and while there are proponents of this theory, even today, the stand taken all those years ago by the AKC remains unchanged. However, one thing has changed. The Miniature Dachshund no longer is considered the "stepchild" of his Standard counterpart! This is thanks to the many breeders of Miniature Dachshunds down through the years who have worked hard and have made continuous improvement in all three varieties of the breed.

One cannot talk about Dachshunds in America without mentioning Fred and Rose Heying and their contribution to the breed. They lived in California and had been breeding since the 1920s, but it was in 1945 that the Heyings purchased a dog from the Josef and Marie Mehrers' Marienlust Kennels. Josef had named that puppy Favorite, and he was shown as Favorite v. Marienlust.

It is impossible to measure the impact that the Heyings' dog Favorite made upon the breed. He is behind most of the smooth Dachshunds in America, and at the time of his death, he had ninety-five champions.

Another breeder, Mr. John Cook (who was later known as "Mr. Dachshund"), began his famous Kleetal strain of smooth Standards. His kennels were extensive and his knowledge of the breed likewise. It is impossible to include all of the kennels and people who made such an active contribution to make this little hound an ever-popular resident in the dog world.

IN THE LIMELIGHT

Because of the adaptability of this little hound who thinks big and has such an alert, intelligent outlook on life, the Dachshund has had his share of the "good life."

The Ugly Dachshund, a Walt Disney film available on video, shows how three or four of these hounds take charge of one Great Dane, causing havoc along the way.

Another Miniature Dachshund was a major player in Tom Wolfe's novel, *The Bonfire of the Vanities,* and appeared in the movie role. In *Once Upon a Crime,* starring the late John Candy, two red smooth Dachshunds add a touch of comic relief and are a major part of the plot.

Dachshunds are judged as part of the Hound Group.

As you can see, the Dachshund has survived through the centuries due to the dedication of the many breeders and owners who persevered to make this dog what he is today. He is used successfully in the field; he is at home in the show ring, where he does a great deal of winning in all coats and both sizes; and he is active in the obedience ring. He competes in den trials as well as field trials, and it does seem that the strife of earlier times, which split the breed into two sectors—field and show ring—has found common ground. It is not uncommon for a dog to do both. There are many dual champions.

FAMOUS OWNERS OF DACHSHUNDS

Pablo Picasso

John Wayne

Clark Gable

Andy Warhol

Paulette Goddard

Liz Smith

E.B. White

Errol Flynn

Carole Lombard

William Randolph Hearst

65

The Dachshund's wise expression and spunky attitude has made him an all-around favorite.

CHAPTER EIGHT

On Good Behavior

by Ian Dunbar, Ph.D., MRCVS

BASIC TRAINING FOR OWNERS

Ideally, basic owner training should begin well before you select your dog. Find out all you can about your chosen breed first, then master rudimentary training and handling skills. If you already have your puppy-dog, owner training is a dire emergency—the clock is ticking! Especially for puppies, the first few weeks at home are the most important and influential days in the dog's life. Indeed, the cause of most adolescent and adult problems may be traced back to the initial days the pup explores her new home. This is the time to establish the *status quo*—to teach the puppydog how you would like her to behave and so prevent otherwise quite predictable problems.

In addition to consulting breeders and breed books such as this one (which understandably have a positive breed bias), seek out as many pet owners with your breed as you can find. Good points are obvious. What you want to find out are the breed-specific problems, so you can nip them in the bud. In particular, you should talk to owners with adolescent dogs and make a list of all anticipated problems. Most important, test drive at least half a dozen adolescent and adult dogs of your breed yourself. An 8-week-old puppy is deceptively easy to handle, but she will acquire adult size, speed and strength in just four months, so you should learn now what to prepare for.

Puppy and pet dog training classes offer a convenient venue to locate pet owners and observe dogs in action. For a list of suitable trainers in your area, contact the Association of Pet Dog Trainers (see chapter 9). You may also begin your basic owner training by observing other owners in class. Watch as many classes and test drive as many dogs as possible. Select an upbeat, dog-friendly, people-friendly, fun-and-games, puppydog pet training class to learn the ropes. Also, watch training videos and read training books. You must find out what to do and how to do it *before* you have to do it.

PRINCIPLES OF TRAINING

Most people think training comprises teaching the dog to do things such as sit, speak and roll over, but even a 4-week-old pup knows how to do these things already. Instead, the first step in training involves teaching the dog human words for each dog behavior and activity and for each aspect of the dog's environment. That way you, the owner, can more easily participate in the dog's

A well-trained Dachshund is a pleasure to live with.

domestic education by directing her to perform specific actions appropriately, that is, at the right time, in the right place and so on. Training opens communication channels, enabling an educated dog to at least understand her owner's requests.

In addition to teaching a dog what we want her to do, it is also necessary to teach her why she should do what we ask. Indeed, 95 percent of training revolves around motivating the dog to want to do what we want. Dogs often understand what their owners want; they just don't see the point of doing it—especially when the owner's repetitively boring and seemingly senseless instructions are totally at odds with much more pressing and exciting doggy distractions. It is not so much the dog that is being stubborn or dominant; rather, it is the owner who has failed to acknowledge the dog's needs and feelings and to approach training from the dog's point of view.

The Meaning of Instructions

The secret to successful training is learning how to use training lures to predict or prompt specific behaviors— to coax the dog to do what you want when you want. Any highly valued object (such as a treat or toy) may be

The first few weeks at home are the time to teach your puppy how you would like her to behave.

used as a lure, which the dog will follow with her eyes and nose. Moving the lure in specific ways entices the dog to move her nose, head and entire body in specific ways. In fact, by learning the art of manipulating various lures, it is possible to teach the dog to assume virtually any body position and perform any action. Once you have control over the expression of the dog's behaviors and can elicit any body position or behavior at will, you can easily teach the dog to perform on request.

Tell your dog what you want her to do, use a lure to entice her to respond correctly, then profusely praise and maybe reward her once she performs the desired action. For example, verbally request "Fido, sit!" while you move a squeaky toy upwards and backwards over the dog's muzzle (lure-movement and hand signal), smile knowingly as she looks up (to follow the lure) and sits down (as a result of canine anatomical engineering), then praise her to distraction ("Gooood Fido!"). Squeak the toy, offer a training treat and give your dog and yourself a pat on the back.

Being able to elicit desired responses over and over enables the owner to reward the dog over and over. Consequently, the dog begins to think training is fun. For example, the more the dog is rewarded for sitting, the more she enjoys sitting. Eventually the dog comes to realize that, whereas most sitting is appreciated, sitting immediately upon request usually prompts especially enthusiastic praise and a slew of high-level rewards. The dog begins to sit on cue much of the time, showing that she is starting to grasp the meaning of the owner's verbal request and hand signal.

TRAINER'S TOOLS

Many training books extol the virtues of a vast array of training paraphernalia and electronic and metallic gizmos, most of which are designed for canine restraint, correction and punishment, rather than for actual facilitation of doggy education. In reality, most effective training tools are not found in stores; they come from within ourselves. In addition to a willing dog, all you really need is a functional human brain, gentle hands, a loving heart and a good attitude.

In terms of equipment, all dogs do require a quality buckle collar to sport dog tags and to attach the leash (for safety and to comply with local leash laws). Hollow chew toys (like Kongs or sterilized longbones) and a dog bed or collapsible crate are musts for housetraining. Three additional tools are required:

1. specific lures (training treats and toys) to predict and prompt specific desired behaviors;

2. rewards (praise, affection, training treats and toys) to reinforce for the dog what a lot of fun it all is; and

3. knowledge—how to convert the dog's favorite activities and games (potential distractions to training) into "life-rewards," which may be employed to facilitate training.

The most powerful of these is knowledge. Education is the key! Watch training classes, participate in training classes, watch videos, read books, enjoy play-training with your dog and then your dog will say "Please," and your dog will say "Thank you!"

HOUSETRAINING 1-2-3

1. Prevent Mistakes. When you can't supervise your puppy, confine her in a single room or in her crate (but don't leave her for too long!). Puppy-proof the area by laying down newspapers so that if she does make a mistake, it won't matter.

2. Teach Where. Take your puppy to the spot you want her to use every hour.

3. When she goes, praise her profusely and give her three favorite treats.

HOUSETRAINING

If dogs were left to their own devices, certainly they would chew, dig and bark for entertainment and then no doubt highlight a few areas of their living space with sprinkles of urine, in much the same way we decorate by hanging pictures. Consequently, when we ask a dog to live with us, we must teach her *where* she may dig, *where* she may perform her toilet duties, *what* she may chew and *when* she may bark. After all, when left at home alone for many hours, we cannot expect the dog to amuse herself by completing crosswords or watching TV!

Also, it would be decidedly unfair to keep the house rules a secret from the dog, and then get angry

and punish the poor critter for inevitably transgressing rules she did not even know existed. Remember: Without adequate education and guidance, the dog will be forced to establish her own rules—doggy rules—and most probably will be at odds with the owner's view of domestic living.

Since most problems develop during the first few days the dog is at home, prospective dog owners must be certain they are quite clear about the principles of housetraining *before* they get a dog. Early misbehaviors quickly become established as the *status quo*—becoming firmly entrenched as hard-to-break bad habits, which set the precedent for years to come. Make sure to teach your dog good habits right from the start. Good habits are just as hard to break as bad ones!

Ideally, when a new dog comes home, try to arrange for someone to be present as much as possible during the first few days (for adult dogs) or weeks for puppies. With only a little forethought, it is surprisingly easy to find a puppy sitter, such as a retired person, who would be willing to eat from your refrigerator and watch your television while

Watch training classes, watch videos, read books, enjoy play-training with your dog and then she will learn to be a pleasant and obedient companion.

keeping an eye on the newcomer to encourage the dog to play with chew toys and to ensure she goes outside on a regular basis.

Potty Training

Follow these steps to teach the dog where she should relieve herself:

1. never let her make a single mistake;

2. let her know where you want her to go; and

3. handsomely reward her for doing so: "GOOOOOOOD DOG!!!" liver treat, liver treat, liver treat!

Preventing Mistakes

A single mistake is a training disaster, since it heralds many more in future weeks. And each time the dog soils the house, this further reinforces the dog's unfortunate preference for an indoor, carpeted toilet. Do not let an unhousetrained dog have full run of the house.

When you are away from home, or cannot pay full attention, confine the dog to an area where elimination is appropriate, such as an outdoor run or, better still, a small, comfortable indoor kennel with access to an outdoor run. When confined in this manner, most dogs will naturally housetrain themselves.

If that's not possible, confine the dog to an area, such as a utility room, kitchen, basement or garage, where elimination may not be desired in the long run but as an interim measure it is certainly preferable to doing it all around the house. Use newspaper to cover the floor of the dog's day room. The newspaper may be used to soak up the urine and to wrap up and dispose of the feces. Once your dog develops a preferred spot for eliminating, it is only necessary to cover that part of the floor with newspaper. The smaller papered area may then be moved (only a little each day) towards the door to the outside. Thus the dog will develop the tendency to go to the door when she needs to relieve herself.

Never confine an unhousetrained dog to a crate for long periods. Doing so would force the dog to soil the crate and ruin its usefulness as an aid for housetraining (see the following discussion).

Teaching Where

In order to teach your dog where you would like her to do her business, you have to be there to direct the proceedings—an obvious, yet often neglected, fact of life. In order to be there to teach the dog where to go, you need to know *when* she needs to go. Indeed, the success of housetraining depends on the owner's ability to predict these times. Certainly, a regular feeding schedule will facilitate prediction somewhat, but there is nothing like "loading the deck" and influencing the timing of the outcome yourself!

Whenever you are at home, make sure the dog is under constant supervision and/or confined to a small area. If already well trained, simply instruct the dog to lie down in her bed or basket. Alternatively, confine the dog to a crate (doggy den) or tie-down (a short, 18-inch lead that can be clipped to an eye hook in the baseboard near her bed). Short-term close confinement strongly inhibits urination and defecation, since the dog does not want to soil her sleeping area. Thus, when you release the puppydog each hour, she will definitely need to urinate immediately and defecate every third or fourth hour. Keep the dog confined to her doggy den and take her to her intended toilet area each hour, every hour and on the hour. When taking

The success of housetraining depends on your ability to predict when it's time for your dog to relieve herself.

your dog outside, instruct her to sit quietly before opening the door— she will soon learn to sit by the door when she needs to go out!

Teaching Why

Being able to predict when the dog needs to go enables the owner to be on the spot to praise and reward the dog. Each hour, hurry the dog to the intended toilet area in the yard, issue the appropriate instruction ("Go pee!" or "Go poop!"), then give the dog three to four minutes to produce.

Praise and offer a couple of training treats when successful. The treats are important because many people fail to praise their dogs with feeling . . . and housetraining is hardly the time for understatement. So either loosen up and enthusiastically praise that dog: "Wuzzzer-wuzzer-wuzzer, hoooser good wuffer den? Hoooo went pee for Daddy?" Or say "Good dog!" as best you can and offer the treats for effect.

Following elimination is an ideal time for a spot of play-training in the yard or house. Also, an empty dog may be allowed greater freedom around the house for the next half hour or so, just as long as you keep an eye out to make sure she does not get into other kinds of mischief. If you are preoccupied and cannot pay full attention, confine the dog to her doggy den once more to enjoy a peaceful snooze or to play with her many chew toys.

If your dog does not eliminate within the allotted time outside—no biggie! Back to her doggy den, and then try again after another hour.

As I own large dogs, I always feel more relaxed walking an empty dog, knowing that I will not need to finish our stroll weighted down with bags of feces!

Beware of falling into the trap of walking the dog to get her to eliminate. The good ol' dog walk is such an enormous highlight in the dog's life that it represents the single biggest potential reward in domestic dogdom. However, when in a hurry, or during inclement weather, many owners abruptly terminate the walk the moment the dog has done her business. This, in effect, severely punishes the dog for doing the right thing, in the right place at the right time. Consequently, many dogs become strongly inhibited from eliminating outdoors because they know it will signal an abrupt end to an otherwise thoroughly enjoyable walk.

Instead, instruct the dog to relieve herself in the yard prior to going for a walk. If you follow the above instructions, most dogs soon learn to eliminate on cue. As soon as the dog eliminates, praise (and offer a treat or two)—"Good dog! Let's go walkies!" Use the walk as a reward for eliminating in the yard. If the dog does not go, put her back in her doggy den and think about a walk later on. You will find with a "No feces—no walk" policy, your dog will become one of the fastest defecators in the business.

If you do not have a backyard, instruct the dog to eliminate right outside your front door prior to the walk. Not only will this facilitate clean up and disposal of the feces in your own trash can but, also, the walk may again be used as a colossal reward.

CHEWING AND BARKING

Short-term close confinement also teaches the dog that occasional quiet moments are a reality of domestic living. Your puppydog is extremely impressionable during her first few weeks at home. Regular confinement at this time soon exerts a calming influence over the dog's personality. Remember, once the dog is house-trained and calmer, there will be a whole lifetime ahead for the dog to enjoy full run of the house and garden. On the other hand, by letting the newcomer have unrestricted access to the entire household and allowing her to run willy-nilly, she will most certainly develop a bunch of behavior problems in short order, no doubt necessitating confinement later in life. It would not be fair to remedially restrain and confine a dog you have trained, through neglect, to run free.

TOYS THAT EARN THEIR KEEP

To entertain even the most distracted of dogs, while you're home or away, have a selection of the following toys on hand: hollow chew toys (like Kongs, sterilized hollow longbones and cubes or balls that can be stuffed with kibble). Smear peanut butter or honey on the inside of the hollow toy or bone and stuff the bone with kibble and your dog will think of nothing else but working the object to get at the food. Great to take your dog's mind off the fact that you've left the house.

When confining the dog, make sure she always has an impressive array of suitable chew toys. Kongs and sterilized longbones (both readily available from pet stores) make the best chew toys, since they are hollow and may be stuffed with treats to heighten the dog's interest. For example, by stuffing the little hole at the top of a Kong with a small piece of freeze-dried liver, the dog will not want to leave it alone.

Remember, treats do not have to be junk food and they certainly should not represent extra calories. Rather, treats should be part of each dog's regular daily diet: Some food may be served in the dog's bowl for breakfast and dinner, some food may be used as training treats, and some food may be used for stuffing chew toys. I regularly stuff my dogs' many Kongs with different shaped biscuits and kibble. The kibble seems to fall out fairly easily, as do the oval-shaped biscuits, thus rewarding the dog instantaneously for checking out the chew toys. The bone-shaped biscuits fall out after a while, rewarding the dog for worrying at the chew toy. But the triangular biscuits never come out. They remain inside the Kong as lures, maintaining the dog's fascination with her chew toy. To further focus the dog's interest, I always make sure to flavor the triangular biscuits by rubbing them with a little cheese or freeze-dried liver.

If stuffed chew toys are reserved especially for times the dog is confined, the puppydog will soon learn to enjoy quiet moments in her doggy den and she will quickly develop a chew-toy habit—a good habit! This is a simple autoshaping process; all the owner has to do is set up the situation and the dog all but trains herself—easy and effective. Even when the dog is given run of the house, her first inclination will be to indulge her rewarding chew-toy habit rather than destroy less-attractive household articles, such as curtains, carpets, chairs and compact disks. Similarly, a chew-toy chewer will be less inclined to scratch and chew herself excessively. Also, if the dog busies herself as a recreational chewer, she will be less inclined to develop into a recreational barker or digger when left at home alone.

Stuff a number of chew toys whenever the dog is left confined and remove the extra-special-tasting treats when you return. Your dog will now amuse herself with her chew toys before falling asleep and then resume playing with her chew toys when she expects you to return. Since most owner-absent misbehavior happens right after you leave and right before your expected return, your puppydog will now be conveniently preoccupied with her chew toys at these times.

COME AND SIT

Most puppies will happily approach virtually anyone, whether called or not; that is, until they collide with adolescence and develop other more important doggy interests, such

To teach come, call your dog, open your arms as a welcoming signal, wave a toy or a treat and praise for every step in your direction.

as sniffing a multiplicity of exquisite odors on the grass. Your mission, Mr./Ms. Owner, is to teach and reward the pup for coming reliably, willingly and happily when called—and you have just three months to get it done. Unless adequately reinforced, your puppy's tendency to approach people will self-destruct by adolescence.

Call your dog ("Fido, come!"), open your arms (and maybe squat down) as a welcoming signal, waggle a treat or toy as a lure and reward the puppydog when she comes running. Do not wait to praise the dog until she reaches you—she may come 95 percent of the way and then run off after some distraction. Instead, praise the dog's first step towards you and continue praising

enthusiastically for every step she takes in your direction.

When the rapidly approaching puppy dog is three lengths away from impact, instruct her to sit ("Fido, sit!") and hold the lure in front of you in an outstretched hand to prevent her from hitting you mid-chest and knocking you flat on your back! As Fido decelerates to nose the lure, move the treat upwards and backwards just over her muzzle with an upwards motion of your extended arm (palm-upwards). As the dog looks up to follow the lure, she will sit down (if she jumps up, you are holding the lure too high). Praise the dog for sitting. Move backwards and call her again. Repeat this many times over, always praising when Fido comes and sits; on occasion, reward her.

For the first couple of trials, use a training treat both as a lure to entice the dog to come and sit and as a reward for doing so. Thereafter, try to use different items as lures and rewards.

Instruct every family member, friend and visitor how to get the dog to come and sit. Invite people over for a series of pooch parties; do not keep the pup a secret—let other people enjoy this puppy, and let the pup enjoy other people. Puppydog parties are not only fun, they easily attract a lot of people to help you train your dog. Unless you teach your dog how to meet people, that is, to sit for greetings, no doubt the dog will resort to jumping up. Then you and the visitors will get annoyed, and the dog will be punished. This is not fair. Send out those invitations for puppy parties and teach your dog to be mannerly and socially acceptable.

Even though your dog quickly masters obedient recalls in the house, her reliability may falter when playing in the backyard or local park. Ironically, it is the owner who has unintentionally trained the dog not to respond in these instances. By allowing the dog to play and run around and otherwise have a good time, but then to call the dog to put her on leash to take her home, the dog quickly learns playing is fun but training is a drag. Thus, playing in the park becomes a severe distraction, which works against training. Bad news!

SIT, DOWN, STAND AND ROLLOVER

Teaching the dog a variety of body positions is easy for owner and dog, impressive for spectators and extremely useful for all. Using lure-reward techniques, it is possible to train several positions at once to verbal commands or hand signals (which impress the socks off onlookers).

Sit and down—the two control commands—prevent or resolve nearly a hundred behavior problems. For example, if the dog happily and obediently sits or lies down when requested, she cannot jump on visitors, dash out the front door, run around and chase her tail, pester other dogs, harass cats or annoy family, friends or strangers. Additionally, "Sit" or "Down" are the best emergency commands for off-leash control.

It is easier to teach and maintain a reliable sit than maintain a reliable recall. Sit is the purest and simplest of commands—either the dog is sitting or she is not. If there is any change of circumstances or potential danger in the park, for example, simply instruct the dog to sit. If she sits, you have a number of options: Allow the dog to resume playing when she is safe, walk up and put the dog on leash or call the dog. The dog will be much more likely to come when called if she has already acknowledged her compliance by sitting. If the dog does not sit in the park—train her to!

Stand and rollover-stay are the two positions for examining the dog. Your veterinarian will love you to distraction if you take a little time to teach the dog to stand still and roll over and play possum. Also, your vet bills will be smaller because it will take the veterinarian less time to examine your dog. The rollover-stay is an especially useful command and is really just a variation of the down-stay: Whereas the dog lies prone in the traditional down, she lies supine in the rollover-stay.

As with teaching come and sit, the training techniques to teach the dog to assume all other body positions on cue are user-friendly and dog-friendly. Simply give the appropriate request, lure the dog into the desired body position using a training treat or toy and then praise (and maybe reward) the dog as soon as she complies. Try not to touch the dog to get her to respond. If you teach the dog by guiding her into position, the dog will quickly learn that rump-pressure means sit, for example, but as yet you still have no control over your dog if she is just 6 feet away. It will still be necessary to teach the dog to sit on request. So do not make training a time-consuming two-step process; instead, teach the dog to sit to a verbal request or hand signal from the outset. Once the dog sits willingly when requested, by all means use your hands to pet the dog when she does so.

To teach down when the dog is already sitting, say "Fido, down!", hold the lure in one hand (palm down) and lower that hand to the floor between the dog's forepaws. As the dog lowers her head to follow the lure, slowly move the lure away from the dog just a fraction (in front of her paws). The dog will lie down as she stretches her nose forward to follow the lure. Praise the dog when she does so. If the dog stands up, you pulled the lure away too far and too quickly.

When teaching the dog to lie down from the standing position, say "Down" and lower the lure to the floor as before. Once the dog has lowered her forequarters and assumed a play bow, gently and slowly move the lure towards the dog between her forelegs. Praise the dog as soon as her rear end plops down.

To teach stand from the sitting position, say "Fido, stand," slowly move the lure half a dog-length away from the dog's nose, keeping it at nose level, and praise the dog as she stands to follow the lure. As soon as the dog stands, lower the lure to just beneath the dog's chin to entice her to look down; otherwise she will stand and then sit immediately. To prompt the dog to stand from the down position, move the lure half a dog-length upwards and away from the dog, holding the lure at standing nose height from the floor.

Teaching rollover is best started from the down position, with the dog lying on one side, or at least with both hind legs stretched out on the same side. Say "Fido, bang!" and move the lure backwards and along-side the dog's muzzle to her elbow (on the side of her outstretched hind legs). Once the dog looks to the side and backwards, very slowly move the lure upwards to the dog's shoulder and backbone. Tickling the dog in the goolies (groin area) often invokes a reflex-raising of the hind leg as an appeasement gesture, which facil-itates the tendency to roll over. If you move the lure too quickly and the dog jumps into the standing position, have patience and start again. As soon as the dog rolls onto her back, keep the lure stationary and mesmerize the dog with a relax-ing tummy rub.

To teach rollover-stay when the dog is standing or moving, say "Fido, bang!" and give the appropriate hand signal (with index finger pointed and thumb cocked in true Sam Spade fashion), then in one fluid movement lure her to first lie down and then rollover-stay as above.

Teaching the dog to stay in each of the above four positions becomes a piece of cake after first teaching the dog not to worry at the toy or treat training lure. This is best ac-complished by hand feeding dinner kibble. Hold a piece of kibble firmly in your hand and softly instruct "Off!" Ignore any licking and slobbering for however long the dog worries at the treat, but say "Take it!" and offer the kibble the instant the dog breaks contact with her muzzle. Repeat this a few times, and then up the ante and insist the dog remove her muzzle for one whole second before offering the kibble. Then progressively refine your criteria and have the dog not touch your hand (or treat) for longer and longer periods on each trial, such as for two seconds, four seconds, then six, ten, fifteen, twenty, thirty seconds and so on.

The dog soon learns: (1) worrying at the treat never gets results, whereas (2) noncontact is often rewarded after a variable time lapse.

Teaching "Off!" has many useful applications in its own right. Additionally, instructing the dog not to touch a training lure often produces spontaneous and magical stays. Request the dog to stand-stay, for example, and not to touch the lure. At first set your sights on a short two-second stay before rewarding the dog. (Remember, every long journey begins with a single step.) However, on subsequent trials, gradually and progressively increase the length of stay required to receive a reward. In no time at all your dog will stand calmly for a minute or so.

FINDING A TRAINER

Have fun with your dog, take a training class! But don't just sign on any dotted line, find a trainer whose approach and style you like and whose students (and their dogs) are really learning. Ask to visit a class to observe a trainer in action. For the names of trainers near you, ask your veterinarian, your pet supply store, your dog-owning neighbors or call (800) PET-DOGS (the Association of Pet Dog Trainers.)

RELEVANCY TRAINING

Once you have taught the dog what you expect her to do when requested to come, sit, lie down, stand, rollover and stay, the time is right to teach the dog why she should comply with your wishes. The secret is to have

To get your puppy used to the feel of a leash, put him on it for a few short trips around the house.

81

many (many) extremely short training interludes (two to five seconds each) at numerous (numerous) times during the course of the dog's day.

WALK BY YOUR SIDE

Many people attempt to teach a dog to heel by putting her on a leash and physically correcting the dog when she makes mistakes. There are a number of things seriously wrong with this approach, the first being that most people do not want precision heeling; rather, they simply want the dog to follow or walk by their side. Second, when physically restrained during "training," even though the dog may grudgingly mope by your side when "handcuffed" on leash, let's see what happens when she is off leash. History! The dog is in the next county because she never enjoyed walking with you on leash and you have no control over her off leash. So let's just teach the dog off leash from the outset to want to walk with us. Third, if the dog has not been trained to heel, it is a trifle hasty to think about punishing the poor dog for making mistakes and breaking heeling rules she didn't even know

existed. This is simply not fair! Surely, if the dog had been adequately taught how to heel, she would seldom make mistakes and hence there would be no need to correct the dog. Remember, each mistake and each correction (punishment) advertise the trainer's inadequacy, not the dog's. The dog is not stubborn, she is not stupid and she is not bad. Even if she were, she would still require training, so let's train her properly.

Let's teach the dog to enjoy following us and to want to walk by our side off leash. Then it will be easier to teach high-precision off-leash heeling patterns if desired. Before going on outdoor walks, it is necessary to teach the dog not to pull. Then it becomes easy to teach on-leash walking and heeling because the dog already wants to walk with you, she is familiar with the desired walking and heeling positions and she knows not to pull.

FOLLOWING

Start by training your dog to follow you. Many puppies will follow if you simply walk away from them and maybe click your fingers or chuckle. Adult dogs may require additional enticement to stimulate them to follow, such as a training lure or, at the very least, a lively trainer. To teach the dog to follow: (1) keep walking and (2) walk away from the dog. If the dog attempts to lead or lag, change pace; slow down if the dog forges too far ahead, but speed up if she lags too far behind. Say "Steady!" or "Easy!" each time before you slow down and "Quickly!" or "Hustle!" each time before you speed up, and the dog will learn to change pace on cue. If the dog lags or leads too far, or if she wanders right or left, simply walk quickly in the opposite direction and maybe even run away from the dog and hide.

Practicing is a lot of fun; you can set up a course in your home, yard or park to do this. Indoors, entice the dog to follow upstairs, into a bed-room, into the bathroom, downstairs, around the living room couch, zig-zagging between dining room chairs and into the kitchen for dinner. Out-doors, get the dog to follow around park benches, trees, shrubs and along walkways and lines in the grass. (For safety outdoors, it is advisable to at-tach a long line on the dog, but never exert corrective tension on the line.)

Remember, following has a lot to do with attitude—your attitude! Most probably your dog will not want to follow Mr. Grumpy Troll with the personality of wilted lettuce. Lighten up—walk with a jaunty step, whistle a happy tune, sing, skip and tell jokes to your dog and she will be right there by your side.

By Your Side

It is smart to train the dog to walk close on one side or the other—either side will do, your choice. When walking, jogging or cycling, it is gen-erally bad news to have the dog sud-denly cut in front of you. In fact, I train my dogs to walk "By my side" and "Other side"—both very useful instructions. It is possible to position the dog fairly accurately by looking to the appropriate side and clicking your fingers or slapping your thigh on that side. A precise positioning may be attained by holding a training lure, such as a chew toy, tennis ball, or food treat. Stop and stand still several times throughout the walk, just as you would when window shopping or meeting a friend. Use the lure to make sure the dog slows down and stays close whenever you stop.

When teaching the dog to heel, we generally want her to sit in heel position when we stop. Teach heel position at the standstill and the dog will learn that the default heel position is sitting by your side (left or right—your choice, unless you wish to compete in obedience trials, in which case the dog must heel on the left).

Several times a day, stand up and call your dog to come and sit in heel position—"Fido, heel!" For example, instruct the dog to come to heel each time there are commercials on TV, or each time you turn a page of a novel, and the dog will get it in a single evening.

A well-trained Dachshund walks calmly beside her owner.

Practice straight-line heeling and turns separately. With the dog sitting at heel, teach her to turn in place. After each quarter-turn, half-turn or full turn in place, lure the dog to sit at heel. Now it's time for short straight-line heeling sequences, no more than a few steps at a time. Always think of heeling in terms of sit-heel-sit sequences—start and end with the dog in position and do your best to keep her there when moving. Progressively increase the number of steps in each sequence. When the dog remains close for 20 yards of straight-line heeling, it is time to add a few turns and then sign up for a happy-heeling obedience class to get some advice from the experts.

No Pulling on Leash

You can start teaching your dog not to pull on leash anywhere—in front of the television or outdoors—but regardless of location, you must not take a single step with tension in the leash. For a reason known only to dogs, even just a couple of paces of pulling on leash is intrinsically motivating and diabolically rewarding. Instead, attach the leash to the dog's collar, grasp the other end firmly with both hands held close to your chest, and stand still—do not budge an inch. Have somebody watch you with a stopwatch to time your progress, or else you will never believe this will work and so you will not even try the exercise, and your shoulder and the dog's neck will be traumatized for years to come.

Stand still and wait for the dog to stop pulling, and to sit and/or lie down. All dogs stop pulling and sit eventually. Most take only a couple of minutes; the all-time record is $22\frac{1}{2}$ minutes. Time how long it takes. Gently praise the dog when she stops pulling, and as soon as she sits, enthusiastically praise the dog and take just one step forwards, then immediately stand still. This single step usually demonstrates the ballistic reinforcing nature of pulling on leash; most dogs explode to the end of the leash, so be prepared for the strain. Stand firm and wait for the dog to sit again. Repeat this half a dozen times and you will probably notice a progressive reduction in the force of the dog's one-step explosions and a radical reduction in the time it takes for the dog to sit each time.

As the dog learns "Sit we go" and "Pull we stop," she will begin to walk forward calmly with each single step and automatically sit when you stop. Now try two steps before you stop. Wooooooo! Scary! When the dog has mastered two steps at a time, try for three. After each success, progressively increase the number of steps in the sequence: try four steps and then six, eight, ten and twenty steps before stopping. Congratulations! You are now walking the dog on leash.

Whenever walking with the dog (off leash or on leash), make sure you stop periodically to practice a few position commands and stays before instructing the dog to "Walk on!"

Integrating training into a walk offers 200 separate opportunities to use the continuance of the walk as a reward to reinforce the dog's education.

Dachshunds, like all dogs, will need to have their abundant energy and curiosity reigned in by efficient training.

CHAPTER NINE

Resources

BOOKS

About Dachshunds

Fogle, Bruce, and Tracy Morgan. *Dog Breed Handbooks: Dachshund*. London: DK Publishing, 1997.

Hutchinson, Bruce, and Dee Hutchinson. *The Complete Dachshund*. New York: Howell Book House, 1997.

Mesitrell, Lois. *The New Dachshund*. New York: Howell Book House, 1976.

Nicholas, Anna Katherine, and Marcia A. Foy. *The Dachshund*. Neptune, NJ: TFH Publications, 1987.

About Health Care

American Kennel Club. *American Kennel Club Dog Care and Training*. New York: Howell Book House, 1991.

Carlson, Delbert, DVM, and James Giffen, MD. *Dog Owner's Home Veterinary Handbook*. New York: Howell Book House, 1992.

DeBitetto, James, DVM, and Sarah Hodgson. *You & Your Puppy*. New York: Howell Book House, 1995.

Lane, Marion. *The Humane Society of the United States Complete Guide to Dog Care*. New York: Little, Brown & Co., 1998.

McGinnis, Terri. *The Well Dog Book*. New York: Random House, 1991.

Schwartz, Stephanie, DVM. *First Aid for Dogs: An Owner's Guide to a Happy Healthy Pet*. New York: Howell Book House, 1998.

Volhard, Wendy and Kerry L. Brown. *The Holistic Guide for a Healthy Dog*. New York: Howell Book House, 1995.

About Training

Ammen, Amy. *Training in No Time.* New York: Howell Book House, 1995.

Benjamin, Carol Lea. *Mother Knows Best.* New York: Howell Book House, 1985.

Bohnenkamp, Gwen. *Manners for the Modern Dog.* San Francisco: Perfect Paws, 1990.

Dunbar, Ian, Ph.D., MRCVS. *Dr. Dunbar's Good Little Book.* James & Kenneth Publishers, 2140 Shattuck Ave. #2406, Berkeley, CA 94704. (510) 658-8588. Order from Publisher.

Evans, Job Michael. *People, Pooches and Problems.* New York: Howell Book House, 1991.

Palika, Liz. *All Dogs Need Some Training.* New York: Howell Book House, 1997.

Volhard, Jack and Melissa Bartlett. *What All Good Dogs Should Know: The Sensible Way to Train.* New York: Howell Book House, 1991.

About Activities

Hall, Lynn. *Dog Showing for Beginners.* New York: Howell Book House, 1994.

O'Neil, Jackie. *All About Agility.* New York: Howell Book House, 1998.

Simmons-Moake, Jane. *Agility Training, The Fun Sport for All Dogs.* New York: Howell Book House, 1991.

Vanacore, Connie. *Dog Showing: An Owner's Guide.* New York: Howell Book House, 1990.

Volhard, Jack and Wendy. *The Canine Good Citizen.* New York: Howell Book House, 1994.

MAGAZINES

The AKC GAZETTE, The Official Journal for the Sport of Purebred Dogs
American Kennel Club
260 Madison Ave.
New York, NY 10016
www.akc.org

Dog & Kennel
7-L Dundas Circle
Greensboro, NC 27407
(336) 292-4047
www.dogandkennel.com

Dog Fancy
Fancy Publications
3 Burroughs
Irvine, CA 92618
(714) 855-8822
http://dogfancy.com

Dog World
Maclean Hunter Publishing Corp.
500 N. Dearborn, Ste. 1100
Chicago, IL 60610
(312) 396-0600
www.dogworldmag.com

PetLife: Your Companion Animal Magazine
Magnolia Media Group
1400 Two Tandy Center
Fort Worth, TX 76102
(800) 767-9377
www.petlifeweb.com

MORE INFORMATION ABOUT DACHSHUNDS

National Breed Club

DACHSHUND CLUB OF
 AMERICA, INC.
Corresponding Secretary:
 Carl Holder
 1130 Redoak Dr.
 Lumbertown, TX 77657

Breeder Contact:
 Jere Mitternight
 2301 Metairie Heights Ave.
 Metairie, LA 70001
 (504) 835-1025

Breed Rescue:
 Emma Jean Stephenson
 (724) 846-6745

The Club can send you information
on all aspects of the breed including the
names and addresses of breed clubs
in your area, as well as obedience clubs.
Inquire about membership.

The American Kennel Club

The American Kennel Club (AKC), devoted to the advancement of purebred
dogs, is the oldest and largest registry
organization in this country. Every breed
recognized by the AKC has a national
(parent) club. National clubs are a great
source of information on your breed.
The affiliated clubs hold AKC events
and use AKC rules to hold performance
events, dog shows, educational programs,
health clinics and training classes. The
AKC staff is divided between offices
in New York City and Raleigh, North
Carolina. The AKC has an excellent Web
site that provides information on the
organization and all AKC-recognized
breeds. The address is **www.akc.org.**

 For registration and performance
events information, or for customer ser-
vice, contact:

THE AMERICAN KENNEL CLUB
 5580 Centerview Dr., Suite 200
 Raleigh, NC 27606
 (919) 233-9767

The AKC's executive offices and the
AKC Library (open to the public) are
at this address:

THE AMERICAN KENNEL CLUB
 260 Madison Ave.
 New York, New York 10016
 (212) 696-8200 (general information)
 (212) 696-8246 (AKC Library)
 www.akc.org

UNITED KENNEL CLUB
 100 E. Kilgore Rd.
 Kalamazoo, MI 49001-5598
 (616) 343-9020
 www.ukcdogs.com

AMERICAN RARE BREED
 ASSOCIATION
 9921 Frank Tippett Rd.
 Cheltenham, MD 20623
 (301) 868-5718 (voice or fax)
 www.arba.org

CANADIAN KENNEL CLUB
 89 Skyway Ave., Ste. 100
 Etobicoke, Ontario
 Canada M9W 6R4
 (416) 675-5511
 www.ckc.ca

ORTHOPEDIC FOUNDATION
FOR ANIMALS (OFA)
2300 E. Nifong Blvd.
Columbia, MO 65201-3856
(314) 442-0418
www.offa.org/

Trainers

Animal Behavior & Training Associates
(ABTA)
(800) 795-3294
www.Good-dawg.com

Association of Pet Dog Trainers
(APDT)
(800) PET-DOGS
www.apdt.com

National Association of Dog Obedience
Instructors (NADOI)
729 Grapevine Highway, Ste. 369
Hurst, TX 76054-2085
www.kimberly.uidaho.edu/nadoi

Associations

Delta Society
P.O. Box 1080
Renton, WA 98507-1080
(Promotes the human/animal bond
through pet-assisted therapy and
other programs)
www.petsforum.com/DELTASOCIETY/
dsi400.htm

Dog Writers Association of America
(DWAA)
Sally Cooper, Secretary
222 Woodchuck Lane
Harwinton, CT 06791
www.dwaa.org

National Association for Search and
Rescue (NASAR)
4500 Southgate Place, Ste. 100
Chantilly, VA 20157
(703) 222-6277
www.nasar.org

Therapy Dogs International
6 Hilltop Rd.
Mendham, NJ 07945

OTHER USEFUL RESOURCES— WEB SITES

General Information— Links to Additional Sites, On-Line Shopping

www.k9web.com – resources for the dog
world

www.netpet.com – pet related products,
software and services

www.apapets.com – The American Pet
Association

www.dogandcatbooks.com – book
catalog

www.dogbooks.com – on-line bookshop

www.animal.discovery.com/ – cable
television channel on-line

Health

www.avma.org – American Veterinary
Medical Association (AVMA)

www.aplb.org – Association for Pet Loss Bereavement (APLB)—contains an index of national hot lines for on-line and office counseling.

www.netfopets.com/AskTheExperts. html – veterinary questions answered on-line.

Breed Information

www.bestdogs.com/news/ – newsgroup

www.cheta.net/connect/canine/breeds/ – Canine Connections Breed Information Index

91

Put a picture of your dog
in this box

Your Dog's Name

Your Dog's License Number ______

Date of Birth ______

Your Dog's Veterinarian ______

Address ______

Phone Number ______

Medications ______

Vet Emergency Number ______

Additional Emergency Numbers ______

Feeding Instructions ______

Exercise Routine ______

Favorite Treats ______

Tear me out!

YOUR

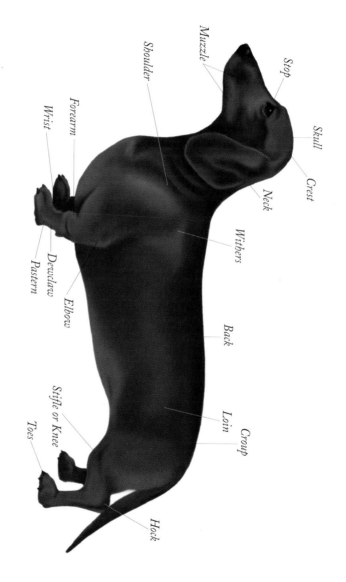

Muzzle

Shoulder

Stop

Skull

Crest

Neck

Forearm

Wrist

Withers

Dewclaw

Pastern

Elbow

Back

Stifle or Knee

Toes

Loin

Croup

Hock